Opera Guide

19

The Mastersingers of Nuremberg
Die Meistersinger von Nürnberg

Wagner

Alberto Remedios as Walther von Stolzing and Margaret Curphey as Eva in the 1968 Sadler's Wells production by Glen Byam Shaw and John Blatchley, conducted by Reginald Goodall (photo: Reg Wilson)

Preface

This series, published under the auspices of English National Opera and The Royal Opera, aims to prepare audiences to enjoy and evaluate opera performances. Each book contains the complete text, set out in the original language together with a current performing translation. The accompanying essays have been commissioned as general introductions to aspects of interest in each work. As many illustrations and musical examples as possible have been included because the sound and spectacle of opera are clearly central to any sympathetic appreciation of it. We hope that, as companions to the opera should be, they are well-informed, witty and attractive.

English National Opera is most grateful to National Westminster Bank for sponsoring this Guide, as well as a new production, in its wide-ranging programme of community service.

Nicholas John
Series Editor

The Mastersingers of Nuremberg
Die Meistersinger von Nürnberg

Richard Wagner

Opera Guide Series Editor: Nicholas John

Published in association with
English National Opera and The Royal Opera
This Guide is sponsored by ♻ National Westminster Bank

John Calder · London
Riverrun Press · New York

First published in Great Britain, 1983, by
John Calder (Publishers) Ltd, 18 Brewer Street,
London W1R 4AS

and

First published in the U.S.A., 1983, by
Riverrun Press Inc.,
175 Fifth Avenue
New York, NY 10010

BRITISH LIBRARY CATALOGUING IN PUBLICATION DATA
Wagner, Richard
    Die meistersinger von Nurnberg = The mastersingers of Nurnberg.—(Opera guides; 19)
    1. Wagner, Richard. Meistersinger von Nurnberg
    2. Operas—Librettos
    I. Title   II. John, Nicholas   III. Series
    782.1'092'4   ML410.W15

    ISBN 0-7145-3961-9

John Calder (Publishers) Ltd, English National Opera and
The Royal Opera House, Covent Garden Ltd. receive financial
assistance from the Arts Council of Great Britain. English
National Opera also receives financial assistance from the
Greater London Council.

Typeset in Plantin by Margaret Spooner Typesetting, Dorchester, Dorset.

Printed in Great Britain by Whitstable Litho Ltd., Whitstable, Kent.

Contents

List of Illustrations

'My most genial creation'

Roland Matthews

'When future generations seek refreshment in this unique work, may they spare a thought for the tears from which the smiles arose! ...'
(Richard Wagner, December 9, 1872; Cosima Wagner, *Diaries*)

To many people the prospect of listening to nearly five hours of music at one sitting is no joke. The conventional wisdom requires that for something to be humorous it must be brief, succinct and possess a quality of lightness, of transparency even; elements, in short, which we do not expect to find encompassed by Wagnerian music-drama, the example *non plus ultra* of extended form and elaborate musical texture. How was it that music-drama could spawn a work that is regarded as one of the greatest comic operas ever written? *The Mastersingers of Nuremberg* appears to be a complete departure from Wagner's previous absorption, in *Tannhäuser*, *Lohengrin* and *Tristan and Isolde*, with subjects derived from myth and romantic legend. Nor was there a tradition of German comic writing for the stage in which *The Mastersingers* might have taken its place. Kleist's *The Broken Jug*, Büchner's *Leonce and Lena*, Grillparzer's *Thou Shalt Not Lie*, stand as isolated examples of a genre that never found a home in the German-speaking world. There were strong local traditions, as with the farces (*Possen*) of Raimund and Nestroy, rooted in the conventions of Viennese popular theatre, but there were no national figures in the comic sphere to compare with Molière in France, Gogol in Russia, or even the dramatists of Restoration England. In the case of German opera examples are just as rare: the works of Lortzing and Nicolai still enjoy a certain popularity in the German-speaking world (Lortzing, in fact, wrote a Mastersinger opera *Hans Sachs* in 1840 with which Wagner was probably familiar), but they offer nothing to compare with the great Italian *opere buffe* of the 18th and early 19th centuries.

It is clear that the compatibility of essentially comic subject-matter with the artistic form in which he had chosen to express his revolutionary theories of the relationship between drama and music was a problem that pre-occupied Wagner in the early stages of the conception of *The Mastersingers*. In a key passage in *Eine Mitteilung an meine Freunde* (A Communication to my Friends), the long essay written in 1851 which forms a summary of his creative life to that point, Wagner seeks to explain why he had abandoned further work in the opera after he had completed a first prose sketch in 1845: 'It is now clear to me why the cheerful mood which sought to express itself in the conception of *The Mastersingers* could not stay with me for long. At that time it was simply *irony* which concerned me, and, as such, it influenced the purely formal side of my artistic views and objectives rather than that core of art whose roots are hidden in life itself.' It is *mirth* (*Heiterkeit*), he goes on, that touches the wellsprings of 'life itself' and that probes beneath the surface to 'that hidden mystery at which we fumble, all perplexed'. This is a distinction which has crucial implications for the completed opera, but it was another ten years before Wagner resumed work on it.

Many commentators would have us believe that *The Mastersingers* was as unexpected a phenomenon in the context of Wagner's artistic development as it is perfect in its construction, a creation that sprang fully formed from his

The First Bayreuth cast, 1888: Theodor Reichmann as Sachs, Kathe Bettaque as Eva ...

imagination, as did Athena from the head of Zeus. But this would be to ignore not only the long period of gestation which *The Mastersingers*, like all his mature operas, underwent, but also the elaborate interconnections which exist between them. Wagner was only too well aware of these links; indeed, he saw his later works as forming a kind of continuum that mirrored his personal development. 'Music has no ending . . . it is like the genesis of things, it can always start again from the beginning, go over to the opposite, but it is never really complete' (Cosima Wagner, *Diaries*, July 23, 1872). Thus *The Mastersingers* looks back to the world of *Tristan* (there is the rare but always telling use of B major, the key in which *Tristan* concludes, at moments when love is under particular strain, as in the lovers' exchanges when in hiding in Act Two and in Sachs's analysis of his own behaviour in the *Wahn* monologue — *'Ein Kobold half wohl da'* ('Some spirit wove the spell'); and further back to *Tannhäuser*, Wagner's first explicit treatment of the relationship between art and life. *The Mastersingers* also looks forward in many respects to the completion of *The Ring* and to *Parsifal*. The development over the years in Wagner's conception of Hans Sachs, his most original, most complete creation, is paralleled closely by the changes wrought on his other great baritone protagonist, Wotan in *The Ring*. Both gain in dramatic prominence and achieve tragic greatness by renouncing a claim that is no longer in tune with the natural order. But Sachs is also an *active* force of redemption and in this respect he anticipates Parsifal who by coming to a full understanding of man's suffering is able to restore order to the world.

Interesting though these connections are, the differences are just as revealing: thus *The Mastersingers* has the most specific setting in place and time among the mature operas (if we exclude *Rienzi*); indeed, it conforms almost precisely to the Aristotelian unities, in pointed contrast to

8

. . . Heinrich Gudehus as Walther von Stolzing, and Josef Staudigl as David and Fr. Hofmüller as Magdalene (Royal Opera House Archives)

the epic structures of *The Ring* and *Tristan*. It is also the only opera which is concerned not so much with man as an outsider, a social deviant (the Dutchman, Tannhäuser, Lohengrin, Tristan, Siegfried, Parsifal) as with man as a social animal, defining himself by his position in society (Walther may continue the line of the outsider, but the psychological focus rests without question on Hans Sachs). An aspect easily overlooked in all the exhaustive analysis of Wagner's works is the *titles* he gave them: it is significant that he did not give this opera the name of Walther von Stolzing, its youthful hero, as he had done elsewhere, nor for that matter did he call it Hans Sachs, but chose instead to highlight a distinctive social *group* in a particular German city.

The most important difference, of course, is that *The Mastersingers* is Wagner's only comic opera (discounting the early *Das Liebesverbot* (*The Love ban*, 1836) as too obviously imitative of Italian models to lay any serious claim to originality). No amount of interconnections can fully account for this venture into unknown territory by a composer turning 50 who had only recently, and after enormous effort, consolidated his artistic reputation with *Tristan and Isolde*. For an answer to this enigma we have to look in two areas: the role of humour in Wagner's life, and the circumstances in which *The Mastersingers* came eventually to be written.

It might be supposed that someone who took himself and his artistic mission as seriously as Wagner did could not have possessed much of a sense of humour. He was, after all, given to intense bouts of self-dramatisation and liked nothing more of an evening than to read from his own works to an assembled company. Yet we must not forget that he did not become a father until the age of 51 (in 1865, just before he resumed work on *The Mastersingers* for the third, and final, time) and that the last 20 years of his life were spent therefore in the company of young children (Siegfried Wagner was only 13

9

Act Two in the original production in Munich, 1868, drawn by Theodor Pixis (Raymond Mander and Joe Mitchenson Theatre Collection)

when his father died). Cosima's diaries make it clear that he was a devoted father with a playful streak in his nature which did not even require the presence of his children to be indulged. We read of him delighting in practical jokes and standing on his head when he was particularly pleased with something. Visiting some friends for lunch in Dresden, Cosima tells us almost as a matter of course, that Richard immediately went and climbed the highest tree in the garden (he was then 57!). There was on occasions a heavy-handedness in his humour, as when he would satirise friends or, more frequently, professional colleagues, and he would often labour a comic metaphor or a pun to the point of tedium. At other times, the humour barely concealed outright malice, spite and *Schadenfreude* over the weaknesses (often imagined) of his fellow humans. The street brawl which forms the climax of Act Two had its origins in a real-life incident in Nuremberg when Wagner, in his early twenties, gleefully took part in the gulling and utter discomfiture of an amateur singer with ideas above his station. All these elements are to be found in *The Mastersingers*: playfulness in the treatment of the Mastersingers' outrage at Walther's Trial Song and in the central episode of the second act, the encounter between Sachs and Beckmesser; heavy-handedness in the fact that this same episode is needlessly long and laboured (especially in view of the delightfully succinct scenes which have preceded it), in the thigh-slapping jollity of the apprentices which rarely fails to embarrass a modern audience when presented on stage, and in their arch comment before Walther begins his Prize Song (*'Alles gespannt! 's gibt kein Gesumm: da rufen wir auch nicht "Silentium!"'* 'None speaks a word, but all are dumb; then we need not call out "Silentium!"'). Finally, malice is present in Wagner's treatment of Beckmesser and the Mastersingers and, although it is toned down substantially from the original conception, it is idle to pretend that it is not there, as some critics, most notably Ernest Newman, have tried to do.

Act Three in the first Bayreuth production, 1888 (Royal Opera House Archives)

The first evidence we have of Wagner's interest in the world of the Mastersingers and 16th-century Nuremberg occurs in 1845, that *annus mirabilis* when Wagner, on a health cure in Marienbad, conceived the subjects of every music-drama he was to compose in the remaining 38 years of his life. In *A Communication to my Friends*, he tells us that he had decided, having just completed *Tannhäuser*, to write 'a comic opera'. 'Just as in ancient Athens a humorous satyr-play would follow the tragedy, so there came to me on that pleasure-trip [the stay in Marienbad] the image of a comic play which could in truth be appended to my *Singers' Contest on the Wartburg* [the sub-title of *Tannhäuser*] as a relevant satyr-play.' He goes on to express the polarity between Hans Sachs on the one hand and the figure of the 'Marker' on the other (the official charged with judging a new song according to the strict rules of the Mastersingers' Guild). In his autobiography *Mein Leben* (written in 1864) Wagner describes how on a walk he got the idea of 'a funny scene in which the cobbler, as the poet-craftsman of the people, uses the hammer on his last to give a lesson to the Marker who has been forced to sing, in revenge for the latter's pedantic outrages. Everything was concentrated for me in the two moments where the board, covered in chalk-marks, is shown around by the Marker and where Hans Sachs flourishes the shoes finished with "Marker strokes" — each an indication that someone has "mis-sung" [not sung by the rules].'

The original conception of the story, therefore, lay rooted in a scene that is almost pure farce and was captured in a first prose sketch (1845) in which Wagner is far more strident in his satire of the Mastersingers and their rules. Hans Sachs, in particular, is portrayed as a character at variance with the other Mastersingers and given to sending up their conventions. There is a strong sense of personal bitterness in his behaviour and wilful malice in his attitude towards Beckmesser. It is evident that one of the main attractions of

Eugen Gura as Sachs and Fritz Friedrich as Beckmesser in the 1889 Bayreuth season (Royal College of Music)

the Mastersingers story for Wagner lay in the opportunities which it afforded for launching a sharp lampoon on the musical establishment of the day. In 1845 (before the première of *Tannhäuser*) he had not achieved lasting critical recognition, but, even when he had, he remained firmly convinced that it was the critics and professional musicians who were his sworn enemies and that only the general public truly understood his work. This somewhat idealised notion of *das Volk* still plays its part in the opera (especially in Act One where Sachs argues that the people should be the final judge in artistic matters) but it is much less prominent than in the first sketch where Wagner set the understanding and tolerance of the people directly against the narrow-minded pedantry of the Mastersingers. Chief among Wagner's opponents was the Viennese music critic Eduard Hanslick. Wagner's original name for Beckmesser in the sketches was Veit Hanslick and it seems likely that the eminent critic got wind of this when he attended, on invitation, a private reading of the completed poem in Vienna in November 1862. In the course of the reading, we are told by Wagner in his autobiography, Hanslick grew ever paler and more ill-humoured, leaving as soon as it was concluded. From that moment he became implacably opposed to Wagner and his music, dismissing the *Mastersingers* Prelude as 'a musical product of painful artificiality and positively brutal in its effect' and describing Sachs's cobbling song as 'suggesting an infuriated hyena rather than a merry cobbler'.

12

When Wagner took up the cause of the Nuremberg Mastersingers again in 1861 he softened the vendetta against the musical establishment. The mockery of the Mastersingers' rules and conventions is still present, but it is of a gentler nature and imbued with a measure of respect for their life-style, however constraining this must be for the true artist. Where previously he had conceived the story as a comic relief to *Tannhäuser*, so now he resumed work on it to escape from the worries of *Tristan and Isolde*, his 'child of sorrow' whose projected first performance at the Vienna Opera had just been abandoned after 72 rehearsals! A poignant similarity between the two works is that both were conceived with the object of being easily stageable and of finding rapid and widespread popularity throughout the German-speaking world. In a letter to his publisher Schott of October 1861 Wagner writes of his idea for a 'popular comic opera . . . with the jovial-poetic Hans Sachs as hero . . . the music light in style, easily staged and demanding neither a so-called first tenor nor a great tragic soprano.' *The Mastersingers* may have had better fortune than *Tristan and Isolde* in coming to the stage a mere eight months after its completion (nearly *six years* in the case of *Tristan*) and in winning immediate popularity, but it proved to be far from easy to stage: in the first place it was the longest opera ever written, requiring a massive orchestra; and a good tenor and soprano *were* necessary, to say nothing of the exceptionally long and demanding bass-baritone role.

We have seen already how Wagner recognised the limitations of a purely 'ironic' treatment of this subject-matter. By 1861 his introduction to the philosophy of Schopenhauer and to the principles of the Buddhist religion had given him deeper insights into human behaviour and experience so that his opera about the Mastersingers gained important new dimensions far removed from the purely personal act of vengeance underlying the original conception. Through the mouthpiece of Sachs Wagner now developed his philosophy of *Wahn*, one of those German words that is virtually untranslatable but which comprises illusion, delusion and madness (Wagner called the house he built for himself in Bayreuth *Wahnfried*, the place where he at last found peace from the delusions of life). In essence, this was a bold attempt to analyse and explain the phenomenon of irrationality in human behaviour. When human beings are possessed by *Wahn*, Wagner is saying, they act against their own best interests. Thus, so long as Walther remains absorbed in the 'illusion' of love, he will never achieve his object of becoming a Mastersinger and of winning the hand of Eva. In this way we can also make dramatic sense of Beckmesser. '*Ob der Werbung seid Ihr im Wahn*' ('Wooing has weakened your senses'), Sachs tells him in Act Three. The fact is that Beckmesser has been temporarily unhinged by his infatuation with Eva and his obsession with winning her in the song-contest. In a sense, his tragedy is that we do not see what he is like *before* the events of the opera. He is after all a Mastersinger and must be considered capable of delivering an original poem and melody that bear little relation to the absurdities of his Serenade or his attempt at the Prize Song. Like Shakespeare's Malvolio and Falstaff (the subject of that other 19th-century comic operatic masterpiece) and the protagonists of Molière's plays, Beckmesser brings about his own downfall through the blind pursuit of an unrealisable goal. It is a perfect illustration of Bergson's classic definition of comedy in his essay on laughter (*Le Rire*, 1900) as being caused by human inflexibility: 'a certain mechanical inelasticity, just where one would expect to find the alert adaptability and the living flexibility of a human being . . . a comic character is generally comic in proportion to his own lack of self-knowledge'. Sachs realises what is happening to Beckmesser. In the final text he no longer bears a personal grudge against him: '*So ganz boshaft doch*

13

Keinen ich fand; . . . die schwache Stunde kommt für jeden, — da wird er dumm und lässt mit sich reden . . .' ('The man's malice will not last for long; . . . the hour of weakness comes for each one, then is the time when he will see reason . . .').

The critical passage of the whole opera in this respect is Sachs's great soliloquy in Act Three, generally known as the *Wahn* monologue. Sachs, who has been reading in a history of the world, reflects on the roots of human discord and conflict, prompted by the events of the previous night when all of Nuremberg had seemed to erupt into violence. He accepts what happened and acknowledges his own part in causing the riot (*'ein Glühwurm fand sein Weibchen nicht'* 'a glow-worm sought his mate in vain' is a reference to his own frustrated love for Eva). Yet he does not condone the violence (*'Gott weiss, wie das geschah?'* 'God knows how that befell!') and realises that he can and must turn it to constructive ends (*'Jetzt schaun wir, wie Hans Sachs es macht, dass er den Wahn fein lenken kann, ein edler Werk zu tun'* 'Now let us see what Sachs can do, so that the folly may be turned and used for nobler work'). For there is another, positive side to *Wahn* which the artist is empowered to recognise. In this view art is itself an illusion and it is only by fully acknowledging this that the highest truth may be attained. Wagner set out these beliefs most fully in the essay *Über Staat und Religion* (*State and Religion*), written in 1864 (in other words, during the composition of *The Mastersingers*). The artist, represented by Hans Sachs, is able to manipulate *Wahn* and thus restore order to a world thrown temporarily out of equilibrium by Beckmesser's outrageous behaviour.

The violence which lies just beneath the surface and which can erupt and just as suddenly vanish, as in the Act Two finale; the violence which even intrudes into the solemnity of the baptism scene in Act Three when Sachs boxes David's ears as his way of promoting him to journeyman; this latent tension is both cause and effect of *Wahn* and is what Carl Dahlhaus had in mind when he described *The Mastersingers* as 'the brainchild of an untrustworthy sense of humour' (*Richard Wagner's Music Dramas*, London, 1979). In the midst of the great C major fanfares closing the whole work a little figure is given out on the piccolos and second violins which had previously accompanied the crowd's mocking of Beckmesser before his attempt at the Prize Song. Wagner's comedy derives from a scrupulously honest portrayal of human nature, warts and all. The label 'comic opera', applied at first to the sketches, had become too limiting and Wagner removed it altogether by the time he came to produce the final poem.

The Mastersingers is a comedy in the sense that it invites us to contemplate and laugh at the absurdities of human existence, but to do so on the basis of a profound love. Its mixture of serious philosophising and near-farcical effect is peculiarly German and can be traced back to *The Magic Flute*. It was recognised by that most percipient of Wagnerian critics, Nietzsche, when he referred to 'that particularly German humour of Luther, Beethoven and Wagner . . . which is incomprehensible to other nations and which seems to have deserted the Germans of today — that bright golden mixture of innocence, penetrating love, contemplation and roguishness' (*Richard Wagner in Bayreuth*, from *Untimely Meditations*, 1876). Wagner too looked back in later life and saw his opera was 'right for a German: no pathos, no ecstasy, but emotional depth, good humour; I like to think that there is hope on this foundation' (Cosima Wagner *Diaries*, April 1, 1874). It is because that hope is so authentic and so potent that *The Mastersingers* continues to warm the hearts of all who come into contact with what has been described as 'the longest single smile in the German language'.

The Music: A Commentary

Arnold Whittall

The Background

Wagner's main period of work on the composition of *The Mastersingers* began in March 1862 and ended in October 1867. The Prelude to Act One was written at an early stage, but its celebrated opening theme [1a] may well not have been Wagner's first musical inspiration for the opera. He seems to have written the melody for the Act Three chorale [33] even before the poem was completed, and it is perfectly possible that the chorale from Act One, Scene One also pre-dates the Prelude: certainly its first phrase [8] could well have inspired the theme which launches the Prelude itself [1a]. It has often been noted that the Prelude contains no reference to material associated directly with Hans Sachs: it might therefore have been very different had it been composed after the rest of the score. But Wagner's purpose in the Prelude was not to tell the story of the opera in advance — to write a tone poem — but to present a symphonic study of various associated and contrasted themes. The main themes are those representing the rather pompous but undeniably impressive grandeur of the Masters and their art [1a, 1b and 3]; in contrast come the ideas associated with the spontaneous, eloquent romanticism of young lovers who are impatient with convention and tradition [2, 4, 5, 6]; and one associated with the good-natured commonsense of the townspeople who admire genuine mastery as wholeheartedly as they pour scorn on the bogus and pretentious [1c]. The Prelude therefore represents the work's most essential conflict — between Walther's radicalism and the Masters' orthodoxy — but not the process whereby that conflict is dramatically resolved.

One distinguished Wagnerian, Carl Dahlhaus, has argued* that the Prelude forms a symphony in one movement, with main exposition/first movement, contrasting exposition/'slow' movement, development/scherzo and a second development which is both recapitulation and finale. Certainly, although the Prelude is no more 'absolute music' than any of Wagner's other mature compositions, it is still a rich and elaborate musical structure, and symphonic in the way its basic themes are treated as well as in its harmonic organisation, establishing, departing from and returning to a principal key, C major. This key can be regarded as the principal key of the whole work, even though it does not make its presence felt throughout in the way the principal key of a symphony can do. *The Mastersingers* is too extended, flexible and radical a structure to be symphonic in that sense. Nor, at this stage of his career, did Wagner use his themes and their constituent motifs merely as illustrative signals to the audience. They have structural significance for the music as well as symbolic significance for the plot, and may be alluded to for musical reasons when their precise pictorial significance is ambiguous.

Since the Prelude does not introduce all the most important themes of the work much innocent pleasure may be had in trying to show how themes which emerge later might be related to those in the Prelude. The decision about the point at which such activities become futile is a personal one, and will depend on how important the principle of unity is to the person making it. It is

---

* *Richard Wagner's Music Dramas* (trans. M. Whittall, Cambridge 1980)

Franz Lechleitner as Walther von Stolzing (Royal Opera House Archives)　　*Wilhelm Gombert as David (Royal Opera House Archives)*

generally agreed that works of art communicate most successfully if they are coherent; and coherence — making sense by 'hanging together' — implies a balance between similarities and contrasts in which the similarities, the unifying factors, predominate. But a five-hour stage work is very different from a 20-minute string quartet or a 40-minute symphony, not least because its unity will be achieved as much through character, setting and action as through music. In Wagner, as in other opera composers, the stress is less on monolithic unity than on a continuous process of evolution. In this commentary, therefore, the identification of themes and motifs — and the common elements underlying certain contrasts — will be placed in the context of fundamental formal and harmonic factors which, while often not consciously perceived by the listener, are the composer's most basic means of ensuring that he creates something which is satisfyingly constructed, as well as immediately communicative.

Such general points need to be stressed because *The Mastersingers* is probably Wagner's most richly detailed score. A full account of its small-scale form-building processes, its thematic and harmonic evolution, would run to many hundreds of pages. This essay is very much a selective summary, which can barely begin to do justice to such skill and subtlety. And the subtlety, as well as the humour, of *The Mastersingers* owes much to the fact that its main subject is music itself. It therefore depends on distinctions between those moments in the drama when 'real' music is being performed on stage, and those passages where the characters are singing what is, 'in reality', speech. *The Mastersingers* is also about the differences between the old orthodoxy and the new unorthodoxy in music. But although the moods expressed in the score range from mocking wit to deep reflectiveness, from youthful exuberance to high romance, it is all — even Beckmesser's distracted strummings on his lute — composed within the orbit of Wagner's own style. The work is not a

16

documentary about a 16th-century conflict between incompatible concepts of what music should be despite references to an actual Mastersong [3]. Every note is Wagner's, and in his dream-like display of compositional virtuosity, the aesthetic and social issues resonate more profoundly and memorably than they ever would in a soberly historical treatment of the same dramatic theme.

Act One

The first scene of Act One is usually passed over relatively rapidly in brief descriptions of the work, on the grounds that it is preliminary, and that only in the second scene, with David's extended account of the Mastersingers' rules and regulations, does the drama really begin. But Scene One is crucial, not only because it establishes the work's pervasive lightness of tone and touch — such pace is a vital component of comedy, especially so extended a comedy — but because the flexible continuity of its organisation perfectly matches the spontaneous appeal of the music. Wagner's actual material may not always seem particularly inspired or compelling in itself: it's not difficult to argue that Mozart or Schubert are greater melodists. But the material becomes compelling through the way it is used, and its utter appropriateness for its dramatic purpose. The most essential of all Wagner's usages — or techniques — is variation, on both the largest and smallest scales. For example, the initial chorale, with its 'romantic' interpolations, offers a fascinating blend of contrast and similarity; and in purely melodic terms, perhaps, the second phrase of [8] is as much a relative of the first as a complement to it. After the chorale, the second part of the scene is built around three objects which Eva and Magdalene have mislaid — kerchief, brooch and book. Each time Magdalene goes in search of one of them the same musical material is heard, in related, varied guise, and this is a form-building process which can function whether or not the material in question is one of the work's more prominent themes or not — in this case, it is not. As Scene One proceeds, it offers a vivid portrait of Walther's barely restrained impulsiveness — he cannot help being 'in breach of custom' — and the most substantial musical focus is a busy version of [1a], which underpins the preliminary discussion of the nature of mastery, and shows to perfection how voice and orchestra combine to create the musical substance. Thematic statement may be more complete, thematic development more intense, in the orchestra: but the vocal line itself is shaped to ensure that the expressive focus of the music is with the character represented on stage. The vocal line is never merely incidental.

At the end of this scene, there is no doubt about the wholeheartedness with which both Walther and Eva identify with the Prelude's main love theme [5]. However, the rest of Act One is less immediately concerned with love than with the nature of mastery as defined by the Masters' own rules, and the quality of Walther's art, which seems to flout those rules at every turn. The music of Scene Two retains the essentially light quality of Scene One, as David relishes every detail of the various poetic and musical laws. The opening phrase of David's exposition derives its descending line [10] from the theme to which he first appeared [9]: and a still more elaborately decorated descending shape provides the scene's most eloquent phrase [12] — by which time the connection between the idea of a new Mastersong and Walther's own love theme is being made clear [z in 5 and 12]. Some may even see a connection between all these ideas and the tune which is heard after David's first mention of Hans Sachs [11]: but Sachs's 'working' theme, to which David describes his Master's tendency to take the strap to his apprentice, is rather differently shaped [22a]. The musical and dramatic effectiveness of David's long solo — structured by Wagner with a throughcomposed mastery remote from the

Thomas Hemsley as Beckmesser with Gwynne Howell as Pogner at ENO (photo: Reg Wilson)

procedural restrictions it describes — is strengthened by the increasingly frequent interruptions. Walther's comments ensure that his ardent musical character is not forgotten, and the most extended contributions of the apprentices frame David's references to a second character who has yet to be seen: Beckmesser. Wagner later develops Beckmesser's main motif [18b] from the little descending figure heard here [18a].

The whole of David's solo is structured around the tonality of D major, with B flat as the main area of contrast, and the tonality shifts from D to a close relative, G, for the apprentices' ensemble. Now, as the Masters themselves approach, there is a more extreme shift to the key of F, which will function for large parts of the long third scene. This scene contains at least seven distinct stages, and a good deal of new thematic material. First comes the assembly of the Masters, an episode whose gradual, cumulative progress is achieved by allowing a single broad yet lively theme to dominate it [14]. The effect is not unlike that of a chaconne. One can see why Wagner thought of Bach, the master of cumulative design as well as of contrapuntal artifice, in connection with *The Mastersingers*; and Wagner's own polyphonic skill at fitting x from [1a] and x from [2] to [14] is no less impressive for its apparent effortlessness. After Sachs's entrance, the roll-call is set to a concentrated recapitulation of the assembly music, a variation which focuses more closely than the original on its basic F major harmony.

Pogner's address shares both tonality and time-signature with the assembly music, but it has a new theme [15], an idea whose main motif — x in [15] — is in essence little more than the elaboration of a single triad, and which for that very reason is especially useful for development in complex ensembles. As he proceeds, Pogner himself describes the importance of the Masters' art [x from 1a], and in the recapitulatory final section (a concentrated variant of the first, far from an exact repetition) the main motifs of [14] and [15] are combined. The Masters' excited discussion of Pogner's proposal appropriately develops x from [15], while Sachs's calming intervention concentrates on x from [1a] —

The trial song at Bayreuth in Wolfgang Wagner's 1981 production (photo: Festspiele Bayreuth)

the Masters' art as something which all the people can recognise and appreciate.

Much of the important new material to be introduced in the remainder of the act is associated with Walther: a 'theme of knightly character' [16a] as he enters to be presented to the assembly, and ideas from his two extended solos [16b, 19 and 16c, the latter close to 6]. Of the other ideas, that are associated with Sachs's sympathy for Walther [22b] will be particularly important later in the work: so will be the music for Beckmesser's anger and malice [18b and 20].

Walther's first solo has three related sections, separated by dialogue which anticipates the disputes to come; and it is the third section which is the most radical in its treatment of the basic material, although it regains its main key of D major well before the end. After the broad comedy of Kothner's reading of the rules [with x from 1a prominent], and Beckmesser's preparations for his duties [18b], Walther's trial song begins impulsively and expansively, and provokes not only interruptions but a complex ensemble which underpins, and undermines, its final stages. The first part of the song has three sections — an ABA[1] form — and the second part, when Walther is eventually allowed to begin it, after Beckmesser's tirade and Sachs's attempt at arbitration, starts with its 'B' section, proceeding to an 'A[2]' which unfolds over the welter of comment and complaint from the Masters. When Wagner adds the apprentices' song to the texture the individual strands are woven into a rich blend which drives the music to its main concluding cadence, at Walther's furious exit. But the orchestral music which ends the act is not mere tumult. Wagner provides the essential image for the rest of the work in showing Sachs absorbed by a purely musical idea — [17], a version of [16c] — one which depends for its effect as much on harmony as melody. Sachs is at odds with his colleagues and the contrast between [17] and what now seems a derisive rather than noble [1a] at the very end of the act encapsulates the opposition which the rest of the drama will explore and resolve.

Act Two

Wagner organised the main climaxes of all three acts of *The Mastersingers* in comparable fashion, as formal 'songs' which evolve, or explode, into elaborate ensembles. In Act Three it is an ensemble of admiration and approval: but Act Two, like Act One, has an ensemble of hostility, as Beckmesser's Serenade provokes, and is gradually submerged by, the Midsummer night's riot. The contrast between the two prize songs of the last act could scarcely be greater: Beckmesser's may mangle the text of Walther's, but its music is a variant of Beckmesser's own Serenade in the second act. In Act Two, however, the main contrast is not between Sachs's Cobbling Song and Beckmesser's Serenade, but between Sachs's own two solos, only the second of which is a true 'song on stage'. The first is a monologue concerned with Sachs's response to Walther's music. The Cobbling Song, in its clear stanzaic form and uncomplicated material, is more like something of which Beckmesser and his fellow Masters would approve, although in its third stanza Wagner introduces an orchestral countermelody [32, deriving from 22b and 21a] which reflects the undertone of regret and sorrow in the text's references to Eva.

One of the major musical triumphs of this marvellous act — perhaps Wagner's most imaginative and, in some ways, his most radical in its rapid shifts of mood and supple tonal transitions — is the way in which more serious or sustained material is seamlessly woven into the predominantly fast and light-hearted fabric. The opening scene focuses on the apprentices' chorus celebrating St John's Day [x from 15] and the exchanges for David and Magdalene make prominent use of Sachs's working, and apprentice-beating, theme [22a]. This material runs through Scene Two but as Pogner recalls Sachs's words of caution about his 'prize offering' the music broadens into a

The second act in Wolfgang Wagner's 1981 Bayreuth production (photo: Festspiele Bayreuth)

20

restrained eloquence intensified by the surprisingly florid, for Wagner, clarinet arabesques, evoking the balmy summer night, and the more purposeful theme for Nuremberg itself [23]. Scene Two begins and ends in the act's initial tonality of G major, and Scene Three starts, as David sets out Sachs's work-table, in the same way as Scene Two. But then a superbly economical transition magically blends [22a] and [17]. In the monologue which follows, Sachs's attempts to work are interrupted by his memories of Walther's Spring Song [19 and 16c as well as 17]. After its first section, the theme of Sachs's later Cobbling Song [29] is clearly heard as a counterpoint to [22a]. But the second section of the monologue begins like the first, except that it is now in the key of F Walther himself had used, and offers a more extended development of the material than section one. A climax [17] initiates the third section, and only for the final quatrain does Wagner introduce a new theme — one which appears nowhere else: Sachs has decided that he approves of Walther's music, but he does not need to continue quoting it in order to confirm his admiration.

The link to the fourth scene is made through [16b], a motif from Walther's first Act One solo. But with the appearance of Eva a new central key, A flat, is established, and with it comes a new pair of themes [24 and 26] which can be connected with both [22b] and [16c], as if Eva's vulnerability, Sachs's tolerance and Walther's passion were all mutually interdependent. With this fourth scene, the sense of dialogue between voices and orchestra intensifies, and the structural framework of the act expands: this is the first scene to include a large-scale tripartite scheme — the opening material returning at Eva's 'Könnt's einem Witwer nicht gelingen?' ('Might not a widower go a-wooing?') — and to use that scheme as the first stage of a still more extended process, including the quarrel between Eva and Sachs, Eva's discussion with Magdalene, and ending only with Walther's entrance. During the quarrel, much use is made of the contrast between [21a, 21b, 22b] on the one hand, and [16a] on the other: Sachs is reluctant to admit to Eva that he admires Walther's music, and she uses [20] to reproach him. As the tension increases, the music is at its most radical in its avoidance of clear-cut cadences, and its deft thematic interweavings and juxtapositions.

In Scene Five the passionate exchanges between Eva and Walther continue to develop the music of the previous scene (especially [16a] and [22b]): eventually, as Walther grows more furious, [1a] and [20] are brought into conjunction. But the climax is one of those moments of extreme contrast which ultimately enhance the continuity (if not the unity) of Wagner's most elaborate structures from time to time. The discord (a diminished seventh) on which Walther's tirade ends could resolve in several different ways, but Wagner chooses the F sharp from it for the Nightwatchman's horn, and the music now moves into B major as the magical Midsummer night's theme is first heard [25]: it is therefore by statements of this theme in this key that the F major of the Nightwatchman's song is framed. The Midsummer night's theme occurs three times in this section, but the B major tonality grows less and less stable as the lovers hesitate over what to do and where to go. Beckmesser's lute contributes to this uncertainty, and it is only Sachs's preliminary hammer-stroke, followed by the first stanza of his Cobbling Song [29 with 11] which fixes the tonality as a somewhat chromatic but relatively stable B flat major.

Sachs's song is simple and direct, but each stanza forms a single span, with much less subdivision and repetition than in the AAB verses which will be heard in Beckmesser's Serenade, and which, for all their faults of detail, follow the formal rules for orthodox Mastersong. In the discussion which separates Cobbling Song from Serenade, Beckmesser grows more angry, Sachs more benign. The most sustained development of basic material [1a] comes at Sachs's *'Darf ich die Arbeit nicht entfernen'* ('Though to your shoes I must keep turning'), in the tonality — E major — which will eventually end the act. And before the Serenade itself begins, there is a brief development of [25] combined with [22a].

Beckmesser's Serenade [30] has three stanzas in G major which are melodically identical, save for the absence of rests in the third. The riot, though principally concerned with quasi-fugal treatment of a motif [31] deriving from the Serenade, also offers a broad development of that tune by the Masters — suggesting perhaps that Beckmesser has performed it often enough in the past for them to get to know it well! Wagner's use of all this material is as imaginative as it is masterly. The climax of the riot matches that of Walther's earlier tirade: the Nightwatchman's horn sounds F sharp, and he sings his song in its original F major, thereby interrupting the smooth progression of the music as it moves gently through its final meditation on the Midsummer night's theme towards its concluding *fortissimo* chord of E major.

Act Three

The first two acts of *The Mastersingers* have a pervasive lightness of touch which is unique in later Wagner. Act Three has great breadth, but there is nothing heavy or laboured about it, and it gives the work a new dimension, the character of a truly epic comedy. It has a deeply satisfying and wholly positive tone, which even doubts about the tricking of Beckmesser, or Sachs's sudden access of blatant nationalism near the end, can do little to diminish. The orchestral introduction expresses the contrast between the resigned, melancholy, private side of Sachs [32] and the satisfactions not merely of writing poetry, but of writing poetry which has a wide public appeal — the 'Hymn to

Anja Silja as Eva and Otto Wiener as Sachs in Wieland Wagner's 1963 Bayreuth production (photo: Bildarchiv-Bayreuther Festspiele)

22

Dawn' [33] which will be sung by the assembled townspeople and Masters later in the act. (A surprisingly gentle version of phrases from the Cobbling Song is also heard.)

Scene One offers a still stronger contrast: David at his most extrovert [9, 31] and Sachs at his most thoughtful [22b and 32]. David's set-piece, a genuine 'song on stage', has an almost hymn-like simplicity [13] — another offshoot of [8]? — but its subtle ABA[1] structure suggests that David has learned something from Walther as well as from Sachs himself. As Sachs tells the apprentice to prepare to be his herald in the day's celebration, [3] appears in its original C major, and this key will be used to punctuate the act at significant points, before providing the basis for its final stages. For the moment, however, it is heard only in passing. Sachs's Act Three monologue is not, of course, a song within the opera, and not subject to the rules of the Masters' Guild. In it Wagner unfolds an evolutionary design of sovereign inevitability. There are four principal sections: the first associates Sachs's own melancholy awareness of the general madness at large in the world [32] with the very different spirit of Walther's Spring Song [16c]; the second moves from a portrait of a peaceful Nuremberg [23 and 34] to a vivid reminiscence of the town disrupted by the previous night's riot [31]; and the third delicately ascribes the entire affair to the devilment of Midsummer night [25, 31]; in the final section, Sachs decides to see if he can turn all this craziness to positive ends on St John's Day, by ensuring that the townspeople come to appreciate the challenging art of the young knight [15, 2, 23]. It is appropriate that this most wide-ranging of Sachs's solo set-pieces should contain an equally wide range of thematic reference within its flexible form: but what prevents it from being a mere thematic pot-pourri is the progress of its harmonic design — at first ambiguous in its hints of various keys — E minor, A minor, D minor, B flat major — but finally arriving at a grandly stable and secure C major.

The main event of Scene Two is Walther's presentation of two verses of his newly-dreamed Prize Song ([7], which indicates possible links between the 'new' first phrase and other ideas). But this part of the scene is preceded by two sections which contain substantial developments of earlier material: the first focuses on Sachs's benevolence towards the knight [21b], and the second — one of the richest episodes in the entire work — elaborates the love theme [24b] in a guise [27] which strongly recalls a well-known theme from Nicolai's *Merry Wives of Windsor* (1849). The exchanges between Sachs and Walther which immediately precede the Prize Song bring these thematic elements together to complete a structure based around the tonality of E flat and its close relative B flat. And although the Prize Song itself uses the work's central C major, the scene as such ends with the return of [21b] and the scene's framing tonality of E flat ([16a] and [23] are also in evidence).

Scene Three begins with an elaborate reworking of Act Two material as Beckmesser pantomimically relives the events of the previous night, and his outburst of rage later in the scene involves further development of the Serenade and riot themes [30, 31]. In the initial pantomime the soft orchestral statement of the Prize Song theme [7] as Beckmesser sees and scans the manuscript is a particularly delightful touch. One brief prickly moment apart, Sachs is entirely benign in this scene [21b], while Beckmesser's song of triumph confirms that he is a man of few ideas by further developing the material of his Serenade [35]. After Beckmesser has rushed out, Wagner rapidly slows the tempo, and the scene ends, as Sachs observes that Beckmesser will deserve all he gets [22a], with a strong reminder of the C major ending of Sachs's earlier monologue [2, 15, 23].

After that monologue there had been a striking shift of harmonic

perspective from C to E flat at Walther's entrance. Now there is an equally striking shift from C to A flat as Eva appears at the start of Scene Four. It opens with the music which accompanied her scene with Sachs in Act Two [24] but, when she begins to complain about her shoes, a theme is heard which will be used extensively throughout this long and diverse scene ([28], perhaps deriving from [6] and [16c]). At first it alternates with Sachs's working motif [22a] to prepare a *fortissimo* statement of the B major Midsummer night's theme [25] Walther appears: then it underpins Sachs's grumbling as the music moves back to C for the third verse of the Prize Song. The outburst from Sachs which this provokes is most obviously concerned with [29] and [32], but Eva's new theme [28], and also [26], are present too. Eva's emotional rejoinder to Sachs rapidly transforms its use of [32] into that reminiscence of *Tristan and Isolde* which Sachs himself turns into a quotation from Wagner [37]. The dramatic effectiveness of this is obvious, and it also provides a brief shift of musical focus away from the main thematic elements of *The Mastersingers* itself. Their return (particularly x of [28]) as Sachs, his good temper restored, summons David and greets Magdalene, is the more effective as a result: and Sachs's announcement of the need to christen a new Mastersong, with its use of the Act One chorale melody (first in D, then in its original C) is one of the most delightful episodes in the work, as subtle as it is simple.

*Hans Sotin as Sachs
with Lucia Popp as
Eva (above), and with
Reiner Goldberg as
Walther von Stolzing (left),
at Covent Garden, 1982
(photos: Reg Wilson)*

The final scene in Wieland Wagner's 1963 production (Bildarchiv-Bayreuther Festspiele)

For David's promotion to journeyman the Masters' motif (x from [1a]) is employed. And the Quintet is introduced by the most magical transformation of x from [28] as the harmony travels smoothly across the wide space separating C major from G flat major. The Quintet itself is a rare inspiration and, as an ensemble for solo voices, a very rare phenomenon in later Wagner. It has a simple ternary form: A (12 bars) for Eva alone, B (13 bars), using the opening theme of the Prize Song [7], and A[1] (11 bars) which reworks the first section; even here the orchestra is not reduced to the role of mere harmonic support, since the concluding reference to [5] is given to the instruments alone. The mood and material of this most exalted moment are gradually dispelled as the long transition to the final scene begins, and the intimate, romantic themes give way in a long, finely controlled modulation, to the 'public' material for the town and the people [1a, 23].

The Guild Songs and Apprentices' Dance are Wagner at his most direct, though plenty of compositional subtleties (especially the use of 'irregular' phrase-lengths) could be instanced: certainly this light-hearted music is never merely perfunctory. With the entry of the Masters, the main material of the first act Prelude is at last heard again in full [1a, 1b, 3] — material which now spans the remainder of the work. But it is Sachs who is the dominant character, and the concerted singing of his 'Dawn' chorale [33] brings him once more to the centre. The passage in which he introduces the song contest begins [32] like a variant of the opening of his earlier monologue, but it proceeeds, by way of [21b] to an extended reminiscence of the Masters' assembly music from Act One [14] and, at the climax, to the theme of Nuremberg itself [34]. The fast-moving version of the 'mastery' theme is the basis for the gibes as Beckmesser prepares to sing [1c], and that song itself is an unhappy variant of his Act Two Serenade [36] whose tonal uncertainty is enhanced by the choral and orchestral commentary. Beckmesser is laughed into silence at the end of his first stanza, and his 'anger music' from Scene Three accompanies his furious exit. Sachs's ensuing explanation [21b] and his

25

introduction of Walther [5, 16a] make fresh use of the appropriate themes, and the entire section settles into the C major tonality which will provide the harmonic basis for the rest of the work.

Walther needs to sing only one stanza of his Prize Song, newly enriched and extended as it is, to win the acclamation of the assembly, and to inspire their participation. Jubilation breaks out, and Pogner steps forward to invest Walther with the Masters' insignia [3]. Walther's rejection is set to a reminiscence of the Quintet in its remote original key of G flat: but the music has returned to C before Sachs begins his remonstrations. It is clearly unlikely that Walther will protest further, and this great final set-piece unfolds and develops the Prelude's final section, the vocal line a counterpoint of the greatest eloquence. The most dramatic interruption of the process, as Sachs warns of foreign threats to German life and art, is pure recitative, without motivic content, though with suitably unstable chromatic harmony. Then the work's thematic progress is triumphantly resumed, with [23] and [34] for Sachs's last paragraph, and his very last line, set to [1b], provides the theme for the passage of development within the choral finale, otherwise concerned with [1a], [3] and [1c].

Inspiration and inevitability combine to conclude a work whose mastery — surely as subtle and skilful a demonstration of technique at the service of expression as has ever been devised — further enhances its power and appeal. *The Mastersingers* is always described as the great exception to Wagner's normal preoccupation with myth and saga. It is certainly evidence of his versatility: but no less than *Tristan* or *Twilight of the Gods*, it owes its impact to a musical structure of supreme strength and conviction, which never ceases to fascinate, and dazzle — even those who devote their lives to its interpretation and analysis.

Geraint Evans as Beckmesser at Covent Garden in 1982 (photo: Donald Southern)

Karl Schmitt-Walter as Beckmesser at Bayreuth in 1956 (photo: Bildarchiv-Bayreuther Festspiele)

Wagner's Nuremberg

Timothy McFarland

In November 1861 Richard Wagner wrote to his prospective publisher, Franz Schott in Mainz, in the hope (which was not to be disappointed) of attracting a substantial advance on the strength of the opera which he had just begun to compose. A few days earlier he had returned from a brief visit to Venice in the company of the Wesendonks where, according to a famous passage in his autobiography, Titian's painting of the Assumption of the Virgin produced in him 'an effect of the most sublime kind' and he immediately resolved to compose *The Mastersingers*. In the course of the train journey back to Vienna he rapidly 'conceived the greater part of the overture in C major with the greatest clarity'. In spite of being written in a period of such intense inspiration, the letter to Schott concentrates on practical matters: the new opera will be on a cheerful and indeed happy theme, and not difficult to perform: 'each theatre, even the smallest, will always have the means of producing [it].' On the other hand, Schott should not gain the impression that he is merely producing a pot-boiler. 'I intend to *offer nothing that is unworthy of me.*' He then continues:

> I am counting on having depicted *the* real nerve-centre of German life and on having displayed its originality, which is also recognized and loved abroad. I remember, for instance, the time when the Director of the Grand Opera in Paris was examining examples of highly original German 15th and 16th century costume with me, and how he sighed and said: "If you could only bring us an opera in these costumes! Unfortunately, I can never use them!" (This by the way!)

What did Wagner mean by '*the* real nerve-centre of German life'? And why, a mere seven months after the scandal of the Paris production of *Tannhäuser*, was he so concerned to lay stress on the work's appeal outside Germany?

The two questions are linked by more than a mere concern with performing rights and royalties. Wagner's nationalism in cultural matters was in marked contrast to his extremely cosmopolitan mode of life, and never more so than in the decade before he began *The Mastersingers*, during which he was in exile from the lands of the German Confederation because of his part in the Dresden uprising of 1849. He had only been free to return since 1860, and in the summer of 1861 he had briefly revisited Nuremberg with its unmistakable mediaeval skyline and the well-preserved old town inside the walls. But it was in Venice that the urge to recreate it in music had come upon him, and it was in Paris in the following winter that he wrote the text, in a hotel room on the Quai Voltaire, from which he could look out over the river to the Tuileries, the Louvre and the Hôtel de Ville. The current of his nostalgia for the German past clearly ran most strongly when he was abroad.

Nuremberg was one of the most potent focal points of this nostalgia, not just for Wagner but throughout the 19th century and beyond until 1945. For the new German bourgeoisie it provided a remarkable symbol of ancient urban greatness, 16th century rather than strictly mediaeval, surviving intact from the idealised heroic age of Albrecht Dürer and Martin Luther. It had been prominent in literature since the youthful Berlin Romantics, Wackenroder and Tieck, scarcely out of school, had visited the city in 1793 and written about it. By mid-century the cult of Nuremberg and of 'mediaeval' Germany in general was sufficiently universal to account for Wagner's referring to it as '*the real nerve-centre of German life*'.

It had also spread by this time beyond the frontiers of Germany. The costumes shown to Wagner with such enthusiasm by the Paris opera director (an episode which presumably took place, if at all, during the preparations for the ill-fated *Tannhäuser*) may well have been made for Gounod's *Faust*, which had had its Paris première in 1859. Most of the scenes from Goethe's play upon which Gounod based his opera date from the mid-1770s, twenty years before Tieck and Wackenroder made their pilgrimage, and they are not set specifically in Nuremberg. But they do recreate a similar milieu, and they point towards one of the most important sources of *The Mastersingers*.

The young Goethe and his contemporaries of the Storm and Stress period sought for, and achieved, a new poetic language of force, urgency and directness, far removed from the elegant and highly stylized rococo and neo-classical conventions of the 18th century. In doing so they had recourse to the 16th century, not only to Shakespearean blank verse, but also to the world of the real Hans Sachs and the plain, direct four-square 'popular' style of his age, which was also the age of Luther's Bible. The main verse-form of this style, known as *Knittelvers*, consists of rhyming couplets with four stresses to the line, a rapidly-moving, flexible metre which can easily slide into a bumpy or jingly doggerel. Goethe used it a great deal at this time, most notably in the earlier part of *Faust*, and also in a poem called *Hans Sachsens poetische Sendung*, in which he evokes the world of the Nuremberg shoemaker-poet, presenting him reflecting on life and art while relaxing in his workshop on a Sunday morning. This is clearly the inspiration for the first scene of Act Three of *The Mastersingers*. The poem contains many other features which have found their way into Wagner's opera, including most of the more obscure allegorical references in Stolzing's prize-song.* Amidst the great variety of metres used by Wagner, the *Knittelvers* keeps recurring as a kind of metrical norm, and greatly influences the shape and rhythm of the vocal line.

In a rather wider sense than is indicated by this one relatively minor poem, Goethe helped to recreate and project the world of the German 16th century. But he can hardly be held responsible for the fact that the 19th century was to take it up in such a big way. Nor can the Romantics, in whose writings and paintings Nuremberg became a symbol of the ideal integrated community of craftsmen, for whom work and art were one. *The Mastersingers* is the culmination of this development but also (as is the way with such things) a turning point. As the temper of German middle-class culture became more nationalistic in the later 19th century, the myth of the Nuremberg of Dürer and Sachs (and, more loosely, of the Lutheran Reformation) became the hackneyed theme of countless pageants, processions, historical paintings and the like. Hans Sachs himself was the subject of about twenty mediocre plays. The virtues of warm-hearted and plain-dealing reliability, of solid crafts-manship and community loyalty were enshrined as the German middle-class virtues and celebrated in 16th-century costume. And as German nationalism became more strident, self-assertive and intolerant, the cult of Nuremberg was assimilated into the ideology of the extreme right, leading finally to the place of special honour conferred on the city in the Third Reich.

Performances of *The Mastersingers*, the German festival opera *par excellence* and the quintessential expression of the 19th-century myth of Nuremberg, played a prominent role in this development. But the work itself

* For a fuller account see Peter Wapnewski: 'Mittler des Mittelalters' in *Richard Wagner. Die Szene und ihr Meister*, Munich, 1978.

Heinz Tietjen's production, designed by Emil Preetorius in 1933, for Bayreuth

deals with quite different matters, and it can be argued that Wagner was no more responsible for what happened to the idea of 'Nuremberg' than were the early Romantics and Goethe, or for that matter Dürer and Hans Sachs themselves. The question is a complex one, and part of the larger and still controversial issue of Wagner's ideological position, with which we are only concerned here in as far as it affects our view and interpretation of the opera itself.

One person who thought that our view of the opera was vitally affected by the developments between Wagner's time and our own was Wieland Wagner. Of all the productions of the first post-war decade at the Bayreuth festival, none broke more radically with traditional practice than did the 1956 version of *The Mastersingers without Nuremberg*, as one critic aptly called it. After 1945 the city of Nuremberg was reduced to ashes and rubble, and the myth of the mediaeval German town which it had come to embody was compromised and corrupted beyond redemption. So, in accordance with his practice of

Act Two in Wieland Wagner's 1956 production, dubbed 'The Mastersingers without Nuremberg'

seeking to lay bare the essence of the work of art, and to cut away all historically-conditioned trappings of the 19th century, Wieland Wagner presented a *Mastersingers* shorn bare of Gothic vaults and gabled streets — denuded, in fact, of the picturesque setting of the myth, which had in his view obscured the real drama.

In its place he emphasized both in the production and in his programme notes those features of the work which seemed to reflect the genuine world of the 16th century. One of these is the theme of St John the Baptist. The action takes place on his feast day and its eve, the midsummer festival of St John's day (June 24) as Veit Pogner reminds us in his address to the Mastersingers (see p. 57). As the curtain rises the congregation is singing a Lutheran-style chorale celebrating his baptism of Christ. Near the beginning of Act Three we hear David, who is Sachs's apprentice in singing as much as in shoemaking, perform his set piece about a Nuremberg woman who took her child to St John to be baptised and named, only to find upon returning home that a child called Johannes on the Jordan was called Hans in Nuremberg (see p. 99). He thus reminds himself, and us, that it is the name day of Hans Sachs, who is, as it were, the John the Baptist of Nuremberg. This is confirmed at the end of the scene, when Sachs assumes the role of Baptist for the new-born Prize Song, declaring that a child has been born and must be given a name, that Walther is the father, Eva and himself the godparents, and David and Magdalene the witnesses (see p. 114). This in its turn points to a major strand in the opera's main theme, i.e. that Sachs acts as mediator and prophet for a new kind of art, the music of Walther von Stolzing, which is a kind of gospel which he must make known to his fellow-citizens and must persuade them to accept. In this way Wagner adapted to his own theme the convention employed by late mediaeval artists of placing the events of the gospel firmly within the setting of the local community.

The name of Eva gives rise to a similar kind of allusive word-play. In the final version of Walther's prize-song (see p. 123) she is both Eve in Paradise, the pattern of ideal womanhood and the expression of feminine perfection, and also the Muse of Parnassus, the inspiration of the artist. Such couplings of Biblical and classical references were common amongst the Christian Humanists of the early 16th century. But Eve is also, for Hans Sachs, the first sinner, who was expelled from Paradise and needed shoes to help her over the rough stones on her path. She aroused the pity of God who ordered an angel to make her shoes, thus instituting the venerable craft of shoemaking by which Hans Sachs lives. He expounds this in the song which he sings outside his house in the late evening while working on Beckmesser's new shoes (see p. 84) and he does this both to frustrate Beckmesser's serenade and also to obstruct the planned elopement of Eva with Walther — a perverse attempt on Eva's part to flee out of the paradise of Nuremberg, in which she and her lover Stolzing, a new Adam, must come to accept their proper pre-eminent place.

Wieland Wagner performed a great service by laying emphasis upon such details as these, which draw attention to the composer's sensitive adaptation of mediaeval and 16th-century conventions of using Biblical material. In a later production of *The Mastersingers* in 1963 he stressed the 16th-century element even more by evoking a type of theatre which the historical Hans Sachs had used, not unlike Shakespeare's Globe Theatre of the same period. In both productions his main aim was to eliminate as much as possible of the 19th century, both its style of realistic, detailed theatrical illusion and its myth of the city.

Nevertheless it has turned out to be no such easy matter to eliminate the 19th-century Nuremberg. Wieland Wagner's illuminating productions helped

Derek Hammond-Stroud as Beckmesser and Norman Bailey as Sachs in the 1968 Sadler's Wells production (photo: Reg Wilson)

to redress the balance in a necessary way, but they were also one-sided. The picture of the urban community which Wagner's opera gives us has a great deal of interest in itself, precisely as a mid-19th-century creation. The domestic drama of the leading characters is interwoven with a series of public scenes which provide a picture of the city, going about its business and celebrating its holiday in characteristic fashion. We see its citizens going to church, relaxing in the evening, and becoming involved in a riot that is not without an ugly side. Their cultural leaders, the Mastersingers, form a singing-guild which has its own complicated rules and prohibitions designed, like those of most guilds, to keep outsiders at a distance as much as to maintain the standards of the craft. The nobleman Walther von Stolzing has to be taught to accept, at least to some degree, the craft-standards imposed by the guild of singers before he can be fully accepted by the urban, middle-class community.

Altogether Wagner's Nuremberg is dominated by its guilds, as the procession of the final scene makes clear. Here the Mastersingers are preceded by the guilds of master-shoemakers, tailors and bakers, all skilled craftsmen serving the daily needs of their own, self-reliant city. Even Veit Pogner, a rich goldsmith who has travelled a good deal in Germany, is a skilled craftsman rather than a merchant, and his fellow Mastersingers all follow trades such as that of stocking-weaver or pewterer. There is not a single real merchant, financier or entrepreneur among them, or indeed in the whole city, as far as we can tell.

But the real Nuremberg of the 16th century was a major international trading centre with great merchant and banking houses, like the Augsburg of the Fuggers at the same period. Shakespeare's 16th-century Venice is such a city, represented by its outward-looking merchants and money-lenders, who are concerned with great ventures and loans, with repayment and interest exacted according to the letter of the bond. Why is Wagner's Nuremberg such a self-contained, rather inward-looking community of skilled craftsmen, quite unlike the historical reality upon which it is based? The question is of great importance, for it links the cultural influences stemming from the Romantics and from Goethe with changes taking place in the fabric of German society,

31

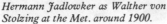

Hermann Jadlowker as Walther von Stolzing at the Met. around 1900.

Victoria Sladen as Eva at Covent Garden in 1948 (Royal Opera House Archives)

and especially in the many venerable cities of the south and west which were seen throughout the 19th century as embodying the traditions of the nation.

Many of these cities (which numbered several hundred, including Ulm, Regensburg and Rothenburg as well as Nuremberg), had been major trading and financial centres in the Middle Ages and the Renaissance, and their greatness rested upon this. But in the following centuries, and particularly after the Thirty Years War, the centre of European trade shifted to the maritime nations of the West, and many of these southern German towns ceased to play a significant role. Most of them were self-governing free cities of the Holy Roman Empire; under the pressure of the times they withdrew into a proud isolation, jealously guarding their independence and striving for economic self-sufficiency as well. Economic progress seemed less important than a well-ordered stability and the preservation of their ancient liberties. Their city councils were dominated by the craft guilds which regulated social and economic life, and in the absence of new wealth they no longer built very much, thus preserving, as though fossilized for the admiration of later centuries, the architectural reflection of their period of greatness.

In this way they survived throughout the 18th century, derided as part of the anachronistic structure of the old Empire by more progressive intellectuals, Prussian bureaucrats, and foreign observers. They seemed to be living survivals of the Middle Ages, whereas in fact they had changed into more inward-looking, defensive communities than they had been before. The other nations of Western Europe, and the parts of Germany ruled by Prussia and Austria, had nothing to compare with them, for their cities had lost their political independence and were being drawn into the administrative structure of the nation-state. The idea of a city community as an autonomous, self-sufficient, tightly-knit community of craftsmen survived into the 19th century in these areas of Germany as it did nowhere else.

But resilient though they were, they could not survive the political and economic changes of the century of Napoleon, Bismarck and the Industrial Revolution. They were all incorporated into larger states such as Bavaria or Württemberg, where they put up a valiant defence of their guild traditions and their rights to self-government. In this rearguard action they were greatly assisted by the Romantic rediscovery and idealisation of the mediaeval urban

Rudolf Bockelmann, an outstanding Sachs, a role he sang at Covent Garden several times in the 1930s. (Royal Opera House Archives)

Friedrich Dalberg as a 'jovial' Veit Pogner at Covent Garden in the 1950s. (Royal Opera House Archives)

community. But, after 1848, they eventually succumbed to the weight of the new German industrial economy, led by Prussia in the Customs Union, and to the centralising administrations of the states. German unification was on the way. In quite precise terms, it was the decade 1855-1865 which saw the end of the old German community-structure of guild economy and restrictions on freedom of citizenship and freedom of labour.*

It is a remarkable fact that the very years during which this massive change in German urban society took place were the years during which Wagner was creating *The Mastersingers of Nuremberg*, a work in which, as we have seen, the central theme of artistic genius and the cultural tradition is presented in the context of an idealised guild of artists in a guild-controlled community. As Walther von Stolzing discovers, there is no freedom for him in Nuremberg until he conforms to the rules. The great procession of the final scene of the opera was presented by Wagner to a German public that was just observing the shoemakers, tailors and bakers of their old towns losing their ancient guild privileges and restrictive rights.

Whether he was fully conscious of it or not, Wagner was in fact erecting an idealised monument to a peculiarly German kind of city at the very moment of its historical disappearance. Out of the ashes of the social reality there was arising like a phoenix a potent cultural myth, of which Wagner's opera is the most complete expression. Everywhere in Europe, a nostalgia for the communities of the pre-industrial age was beginning to emerge at this time, a return to the values of the skilled craftsman in reaction against the new reality of industrial production. But in Germany this nostalgia could be related to a kind of urban community which had survived much later than in the England of William Morris, and in a form which had shaped the childhood experiences of many people.

This is surely the reason why Wagner felt impelled to create a whole urban community in this work, alone of all his operas, and why he was able to claim, when writing to his publisher, that he was depicting '*the* real nerve-centre of German life' in its unique originality. More than in England or France, the nostalgia for the tight-knit local community was to be propagated in the

* For this and the preceding paragraphs I am indebted to the study by Mack Walker: *German Home Towns* (Ithaca, 1971)

Germany of the next hundred years, and seen as preferable to the impersonal abstract role of the individual in modern society. In 1887 the German sociologist Ferdinand Tönnies was to describe the two contrasting forms of society as *Gemeinschaft*† and *Gesellschaft**, and this distinction has remained important for the social sciences.

In a paradoxical way the fundamentally conservative nostalgia for the historical community in *The Mastersingers* is reinforced by the general mood of expansive, patriotic optimism which also characterised Germany in the 1860s as political unification and economic development were seen to be advancing hand in hand. In strict historical terms, the decline of the old was necessary for the emergence of the new; in their cultural reflections, however, such contradictions may be reconciled. One of the most striking aspects of Wagner's genius is his ability to respond to what was taking place in the world of ideas around him, and to project it in powerful images which are rendered valid for the audience by the music in which he expressed them. He had undoubtedly responded acutely to the new mood abroad in Germany in 1860 after his ten years of exile, and was able to weave both strands into his work.

Against this background the story of Sachs, Beckmesser, Eva and Walther takes on a specific colouring. The parable of artistic inspiration and its integration into the cultural tradition, which these figures act out with such warmth and humour, requires a model social community as the final court of appeal. But the vote of approval for Stolzing is not so much a democratic decision by the people of Nuremberg as a plebiscite, a ratification of what Hans Sachs has suggested, helped to shape, and indeed to set up by means of the trap into which Beckmesser falls. The exposure and exclusion of the deluded town clerk is both funny and disconcertingly uncomfortable, rather like the fate of his close relative Malvolio in Shakespeare's *Twelfth Night*. The rejection of Beckmesser and acceptance of Stolzing confirms that Nuremberg is a community open to change and innovation, but reminds us too that the division between those who belong and those who do not, between insiders and outsiders, is as clearly defined socially as it is in physical terms by the city's massive walls and moats.

The sense of belonging to the community is conveyed indirectly throughout most of the opera and is one of the great sources of its appeal. But it too can cloy. Thomas Mann's devotion to Wagner's operas was life-long, but in later years he came to find the atmosphere of *The Mastersingers* oppressive, as he wrote in 1949 to Emil Preetorius, who had designed many Bayreuth productions in the 1930s. Mann now perceived a degree of cosy smugness in the *Gemütlichkeit*, and smelled a whiff of cloaked anti-semitism in the portrayal of Beckmesser. His remarks are similar to the ideas underlying Wieland Wagner's production of his grandfather's comic masterpiece, in that both men were reacting against the inflated role assigned to the myth of Nuremberg, and to its incarnation in the opera, by German conservatives and National Socialists up to 1945.

Those who now come to the opera with the historical perspective of one more generation may not feel able to brush these considerations aside, but neither will they allow the work's place in an ideological tradition to overshadow their response to its warmth and wisdom. It surely increases our appreciation of the Nuremberg Wagner created, and of the characters with whom he peopled it, if we can see not only the cultural factors but also the forces of social change which influenced it, and the end of an old urban tradition for which it provides a memorial and an apotheosis.

† (a traditional community based on custom and familiarity)
* (a modern society based on impersonal legal and economic principles)

Thematic Guide

Many of the themes from the opera have been identified in the articles by numbers in square brackets, which refer to the themes set out on these pages. The themes are also identified by the numbers in brackets at the corresponding points in the libretto, so that the words can be related to the musical themes.

[7] WALTHER

cf 6

Warm in the sun-light at dawn-ing of day, when blossoms rare made the air Sweet
Mor-gen-lich leuch-tend in ro - si-gem Schein, von Blüth und Duft geschwellt die Luft

[8] CHORALE

As to thee our Sav – iour came, was bap-tized in God's own name,
Da zu dir der Hei – land kam, wil - lig dei - ne Tau - fe nahm,

[9]

[10] DAVID

My lord! The Mas-ter-sing-er's way
Mein Herr! Der Sing-er Mei - ster-schlag

[11]

[12] DAVID

The Mas – ter's tones and mea – sures are ma-ny in name and kind,
Der Mei – ster Tön' und Wei – sen gar viel an Nam' und Zahl,

[13] DAVID *Song, Act Three, scene one*

[14]

36

[15] POGNER

The feast of John, — Mid-sum-mer's day, ye know we keep to - mor - row.
Das schö - ne Fest, — Jo-han-nis-tag, ihr wisst begeh'n wir mor - gen.

[16a] *'A theme of knightly character'*

[16b] WALTHER

These now, to gain life's high - est prize
gilt es des Le - bens höch - sten Preis

[16c] WALTHER *Spring song*

[17]

[18a]

[18b]

[19]

[20]

37

[21a]

[21b]

[22a]

[22b]

[23]

[24]

cf 16c

[25] *Midsummer Night*

3

[26]

[27] SACHS

My   friend,   in   joy -   ful   days of youth
Mein freund!   in   hol -   der   Ju - gend zeit

[28]

x

38

[29] SACHS

Jer - rum!   Je - rum!   Halla-halla- he!

BECKMESSER

I see now dawn-ing day – light, that gives me de-light true.
Den Tag seh' ich er - schei - nen, der mir wohl ge-fall'n thut.

[31]

[32]

[33] CHORALE

A – wake! The — dawn – of day – draws near
Wach' auf! Es — na - het gen – den Tag

[34]

[35]

[36] BECKMESSER *Prize song*

[37]

Tris - tan and Is - ol - de

Josef Greindl as Sachs and Wolfgang Windgassen as Walther von Stolzing at Bayreuth in 1963 (photo: Bildarchiv-Bayreuther Festspiele)

David becomes a journeyman in the 1969 Covent Garden production (photo: Reg Wilson)

The Mastersingers of Nuremberg
Die Meistersinger von Nürnberg

An Opera in Three Acts by Richard Wagner

English translation by Frederick Jameson

Revised by Norman Feasey and Gordon Kember

Die Meistersinger von Nürnberg was first produced at the Royal Court Theatre, Munich on June 21, 1868. The first performance in England was at the Theatre Royal, Drury Lane on May 30, 1882. The first performance in America was on January 4, 1886 in New York.

The German text is based on Wagner's manuscript poem as printed by Schotts. Where this differs from what he actually set to music, however, we have adopted the words of the vocal score. The archaic spellings and punctuation, as well as the verse layout, are otherwise those of Wagner's original poem. The stage directions are those in the vocal score and have been literally translated: they do not form part of Frederick Jameson's translation and do not necessarily represent any actual production. The numbers in square brackets refer to the Thematic Guide.

This translation was revised by Norman Feasey and the late Gordon Kember for the 1968 production of *The Mastersingers* at Sadler's Wells. It was then published with the following preface.

Preface

The Mastersingers of Nuremberg is the eighth in order of Wagner's published operas. Some acquaintance with the history of the Mastersingers of Germany, their manners and customs, and their technical phraseology, is indispensable for a due appreciation of much which would otherwise appear strange and incomprehensible in the text of this opera. The Mastersingers are not to be regarded as mythical personages, or as emanations of Wagner's brain, but as real flesh and blood. The aims of the Mastersingers' schools and guilds were strictly moral; by the cultural and improvement of poetry, and by the discipline which their rules imposed, they sought to raise the mental and moral standard of their youth.

In Nuremberg, the principal meetings of the Mastersingers were held in the Church of St Katherine after afternoon service on Sundays and Holy-days. The singing at their sittings was divided into 'Free-singing' and 'Principal-singing'. In the former, anyone, even a stranger, might take part; in the latter, which was competitive, the faults against the rules committed by the singer were noted on a slate by the 'Marker', esconced behind a curtain. Seven faults were allowed, and he who exceeded this number was declared 'outsung and outdone'.

In Wagner's opera, Pogner, the eldest of the Guild of Mastersingers, has offered the hand of his young daughter, Eva, to the Master, who at an approaching public singing-match should win the prize. The Marker for the contest, Sixtus Beckmesser, who has already been paying his addresses to the maiden, finds a rival in the person of the young knight, Walther von Stolzing, who, inspired by reading the *Book of Heroes* and the old Minnesingers, has left the poverty-stricken and decaying castle of his ancestors, with a view to learning in Nuremberg, the art of the Mastersingers.

41

THE CHARACTERS

Hans Sachs *shoemaker*		*bass*
Veit Pogner *goldsmith*		*bass*
Kunz Vogelgesang *furrier*		*tenor*
Konrad Nachtigall *tinsmith*		*bass*
Sixtus Beckmesser *town clerk*		*bass*
Fritz Kothner *baker*	*Mastersingers*	*bass*
Balthasar Zorn *pewterer*		*tenor*
Ulrich Eisslinger *grocer*		*tenor*
Augustin Moser *tailor*		*tenor*
Hermann Ortel *soapboiler*		*bass*
Hans Schwartz *stockingweaver*		*bass*
Hans Foltz *coppersmith*		*bass*
Walther von Stolzing *a young knight from Franconia*		*tenor*
David *Sachs's apprentice*		*tenor*
Eva *Pogner's daughter*		*soprano*
Magdalene *Eva's nurse*		*soprano*
A Nightwatchman		*bass*

Burghers of all guilds, Journeymen, Prentices, Girls, People.

Scene — Nuremberg, about the middle of the 16th century.

Act One

Scene One. *The stage represents an oblique view of the church of St Katherine; the nave is on the left stretching towards the back, with only the last few rows of pews visible: in front is the open space of the choir which is later shut off from the nave by a black curtain. As the curtain rises, the people are singing, to organ accompaniment, the last verse of the Chorale, which concludes afternoon service on the vigil of the Feast of St John.*

THE CONGREGATION

As to thee our Saviour came,   [8]   Da zu dir der Heiland kam,
Was baptized in God's own name,   willig deine Taufe nahm,
Chose to be the sacrifice,   weihte sich dem Opfertod,
For our sins to pay the price: gab er uns des Heil's Gebot:
So must we his children be,   dass wir durch dein' Tauf' uns weih'n,
Worthy of this agony.   seines Opfers werth zu sein.
  Blessed preacher,   Edler Täufer,
  Holy teacher!   Christ's Vorläufer!
Bless us with thy hand,   Nimm uns freundlich an,
There on Jordan's strand.   dort am Fluss Jordan.

During the Chorale and its interludes the orchestra accompanies this mime: Eva and Magdalene are seated in the back pew; Walther von Stolzing is leaning against a pillar at a little distance, his eyes fixed on Eva. Eva turns repeatedly towards the knight and answers his urgent, tender glances of entreaty and passion modestly, but encouragingly. [2, 6a, b, 5] Magdalene often breaks off her singing to give Eva a reproving nudge. When the hymn has finished and during the long organ postlude, the congregation is gradually leaving by the main entrance (on the left at the back), Walther hurries towards Eva and her companion, who have risen and turned to go.

WALTHER
(softly but ardently to Eva)

Oh, stay! – A word! One single word!   Verweilt! – Ein Wort! Ein einzig Wort!

EVA
(turning round quickly to Magdalene)

My kerchief, see! 'Tis left behind.   Mein Brusttuch! Schau! Wohl liegt's im Ort?

MAGDALENE

Forgetful girl! Now I must look!   Vergesslich Kind! Nun heisst es: such'!

(She goes back to the pew.)

WALTHER

Maiden, forgive my bold approach.   Fräulein! Verzeiht der Sitte Bruch!
Tell me but one thing, tell me I pray you,   Eines zu wissen, Eines zu fragen,
For just one word I dare to ask you!   was nicht müsst' ich zu brechen wagen?
If life be mine or death, if blest I be or   Ob Leben oder Tod? Ob Segen oder Fluch?
  cursed?
One single word will my fate decide: Mit einem Worte sei mir's vertraut:
Fair maiden, say –   mein Fräulein, sagt –

MAGDALENE
(returning)

I've found it now.   Hier ist das Tuch.

EVA

Oh dear, the clasp!   O weh! die Spange!

MAGDALENE

Is that gone too?   Fiel sie wohl ab?

(She returns again to the pew.)

43

If light and life, or night and death –	Ob Licht und Lust, oder Nacht und Grab?
Whether I learn the tidings I long for,	Ob ich erfahr', wonach ich verlange,
Whether I hear the words that I dread:	ob ich vernehme, wovor mir graut: –
Fair maiden, say –	Mein Fräulein, sagt –

MAGDALENE
(returning again)

Now you have the clasp.	Da ist auch die Spange. –
Come love, for now you have them both.	Komm', Kind! Nun hast du Spang' und Tuch. –
Oh dear, now I've left my book behind!	O weh! da vergass ich selbst mein Buch!

(She goes back again, hastily.)

WALTHER

The word I crave, you will not speak?	Dies eine Wort, ihr sagt mir's nicht?
The word that will decide my fate?	Die Sylbe, die mein Urtheil spricht?
Yes or no! 'tis quickly told,	Ja, oder: Nein! – ein flücht'ger Laut:
Fair maiden, say, are you betrothed?	mein Fräulein, sagt, seid ihr schon Braut?

MAGDALENE
(who has again returned, curtseying to Walther)

Good sir, I thank you.	Sieh da, Herr Ritter?
We are indeed obliged:	Wie sind wir hochgeehrt:
For Eva's escort	mit Evchen's Schutze
We give you grateful thanks.	habt ihr euch gar beschwert?
May I tell Master Pogner	Darf den Besuch des Helden
That soon you come to visit him?	ich Meister Pogner melden?

WALTHER
(with passionate bitterness)

Would I had never seen his house!	Betrat ich doch nie sein Haus!

MAGDALENE

Why sir, what is this that you say?	Ei! Junker! Was sagt ihr da aus!
Although you've only just come to Nuremberg,	In Nürnberg eben nur angekommen,
Have you not found a friendly welcome?	war't ihr nicht freundlich aufgenommen?
What kitchen, cellar, hearth and home	Was Küch' und Keller, Schrein und Schrank
Could give, does that deserve no thanks?	euch bot, verdient' es keinen Dank?

EVA

Good Lene, ah, he means it not so;	Gut Lenchen! Ach! das meint er ja nicht.
He is only eager to know,	Doch wohl von mir wünscht er Bericht –
How shall I say? – Bewildered am I.	wie sag' ich's schnell? – Versteh' ich's doch kaum! –
I feel as though it all were a dream!	Mir ist, als wär' ich gar im Traum! –
He asks, am I betrothed?	Er frägt, – ob ich schon Braut?

MAGDALENE
(in great alarm)

Oh Lord! Don't speak so loud!	Hilf Gott! Sprich nicht so laut!
Let us now go home my dear.	Jetzt lass' uns nach Hause gehn;
If folk should see us here!	wenn uns die Leut' hier sehn!

WALTHER

No, first give me your reply!	Nicht eher, bis ich Alles weiss!

EVA

'Tis safe, the folk are gone.	's ist leer, die Leut' sind fort.

MAGDALENE

That makes it all the worse!	Drum eben wird mir heiss! –
Sir Walther, some other time!	Herr Ritter, an and'rem Ort!

David enters from the sacristy and busies himself closing the black curtains so as to shut off the foreground of the stage from the nave.

WALTHER
(urgently)

No! First this word!   Nein! Erst dies Wort!

EVA
(appealingly to Magdalene)

This word!   Dies Wort?

MAGDALENE
(who has turned round, sees David, pauses and calls aside tenderly.)

David? Ei! David here?   David? Ei! David hier?

EVA
(urgently)

How can I? Speak for me!   Was sag' ich? Sag' du's mir!

MAGDALENE
(at a loss, frequently looking round towards David)

Sir Knight, the question that you now ask,   Herr Ritter, was ihr die Jungfer fragt,
To answer is no easy task.   das ist so leichtlich nicht gesagt;
Though Eva is betrothed indeed –   fürwahr ist Evchen Pogner Braut –

EVA
(quickly interrupting)

But yet has no-one the bridegroom beheld!   Doch hat noch Keiner den Bräut'gam
         erschaut.

MAGDALENE

The bridegroom's name will not be known,   Den Braut'gam wohl noch Niemand kennt,
Until tomorrow it shall be shown,   bis morgen ihn das Gericht ernennt,
When a Mastersinger the prize has won –   das dem Meistersinger ertheilt den Preis –

EVA
(enthusiastically)

And my own hand will place the crown.   Und selbst die Braut ihm reicht das Reis.

WALTHER

A Mastersinger?   Dem Meistersinger?

EVA
(anxiously)

Are you not one?   Seid ihr das nicht?

WALTHER

A trial song?   Ein Werbgesang?

MAGDALENE

Before the guild.   Vor Wettgericht.

WALTHER

The prize is won?   Den Preis gewinnt?

MAGDALENE

By the Masters' favour.   Wen die Meister meinen.

WALTHER

The bride will choose?   Die Braut dann wählt?

EVA
(forgetting herself)

You and no other!   Euch, oder Keinen!
(Walther turns away, walking up and down in great excitement.)

MAGDALENE
(very shocked)

What, Eva! Eva! Think what you're saying!   Was? Evchen! Evchen! Bist du von Sinnen?

EVA

Good Lene, help now to win me my lover! Gut' Lene! hilf mir den Ritter gewinnen!

MAGDALENE

Yesterday only you saw him first! Sah'st ihn doch gestern zum ersten Mal?

EVA

Even at once my heart was aflame; Das eben schuf mir so schnelle Qual,
Long had I gazed on his portrait fair! dass ich schon längst ihn im Bilde sah: –
Say, is he not like to David there? sag', trat er nicht ganz wie David nah'?

MAGDALENE
(in great astonishment)

Are you mad? Like David? Bist du toll? Wie David?

EVA

The picture I mean! Wie David im Bild.

MAGDALENE

Ah! Mean you the king with harp and Ach! meinst du den König mit der Harfen
sceptre
And flowing beard on the Masters' shield? und langem Bart in der Meister Schild?

EVA

No! He who boldly defeated Goliath, Nein! der, dess' Kiesel den Goliath warfen,
With sword at side his hand holds the sling das Schwert im Gurt, die Schleuder zur
Hand:
His head aglow with locks of gold, von lichten Locken das Haupt umstrahlt,
As drawn by Master Dürer of old! wie ihn uns Meister Dürer gemalt.

MAGDALENE
(sighing aloud)

Oh, David! David! Ach, David! David!

DAVID
(who had gone out, now returns with a ruler in his belt and holding a large piece of white chalk on a string.) [9]

Yes here I am; who calls? Da bin ich! Wer ruft?

MAGDALENE

Ah, David! See how much pain you cause! Ach, David! Was ihr für Unglück schuft!
(aside)
The darling rogue! Surely he knows? Der liebe Schelm! wüsst' er's noch nicht?
(aloud)
Oh look, I fear he has locked us in now! Ei, seht! da hat er uns gar verschlossen?

DAVID
(tenderly, to Magdalene)

Just you in my heart! In's Herz euch allein!

MAGDALENE
(aside, ardently)

How faithful he is! – Das treue Gesicht! –
(aloud)
Come, tell, the reason for this nonsense! Mein sagt! Was treibt ihr hier für Possen?

DAVID

Defend us! Nonsense! A serious thing: Behüt' es! Possen? Gar ernste Ding'!
For the Masters I set out the ring. Für die Meister hier richt' ich den Ring.

MAGDALENE

What? Will there be singing? Wie? Gäb' es ein Singen?

DAVID

Just a trial today: Nur Freiung heut':
The pupil's way will be made open, der Lehrling wird da losgesprochen,
If no rules of the Tabulatur are broken: der nichts wider die Tabulatur verbrochen;
Master may he become with luck. [3] Meister wird, wen die Prob' nicht reu't.

46

MAGDALENE

So then the knight has come here just in time. | Da wär' der Ritter ja am rechten Ort. –
Now, Eva, come! We must go home. | Jetzt, Evchen, komm', wir müssen fort.

WALTHER
(turning quickly to the women)

To Master Pogner let me now escort you. | Zu Meister Pogner lasst mich euch geleiten.

MAGDALENE

No, wait for him here, he soon will come. | Erwartet den hier; er ist bald da.
If for Eva's hand you're striving, | Wollt ihr euch Evchen's Hand erstreiten,
Then time and place are on your side. | rückt Ort und Zeit das Glück euch nah'.

(Two prentices enter, carrying benches.)

Now come, we must hurry! | Jetzt eilig von hinnen!

WALTHER

What am I to do then? | Was soll ich beginnen?

MAGDALENE

Let David now teach you | Lasst David euch lehren,
The rules of the trial. | die Freiung begehren. –
David, this knight must here with you stay. | Davidchen! hör', mein lieber Gesell,
Look after him, and help him well I pray! | den Ritter bewahr' hier wohl zur Stell'!
I'll cook as fine a dish [9] | Was Fein's aus der Küch'
As you could ever wish | bewahr' ich für dich:
And tomorrow your love may be bolder | und morgen begehr' du noch dreister,
If he today becomes a Master! [3] | wird heut' der Junker hier Meister.

(She urges Eva to leave.)

EVA
(to Walther)

When shall I see you? | Seh' ich euch wieder?

WALTHER
(with much fervour)

This evening, be sure! [4] | Heut' Abend, gewiss!
Nought shall dismay me, | Was ich will wagen,
No power shall stay me! | wie könnt' ich's sagen?
New is my heart; new my life. | Neu ist mein Herz, neu mein Sinn,
New now are all things for which I strive! | neu ist mir Alles, was ich beginn':
I know but one aim, | Eines nur weiss ich,
Only this one thought, | Eines begreif' ich:
Doth burn within me, | mit allen Sinnen
How I long to win thee! | euch zu gewinnen!
Without my sword then must I succeed now, | Ist's mit dem Schwert nicht, muss es gelingen,
For as a Master I'll win by singing. | gilt es als Meister euch zu ersingen.
For thee all I hold, | Für euch Gut und Blut!
For thee | Für euch
Poet's love untold. [5a,b] | Dichter's heil'ger Muth!

EVA
(with great warmth)

My heart's love untold | Mein Herz, sel'ger Gluth,
For thee | für euch
Loving thought doth hold. | liebesheil'ge Huth!

MAGDALENE

Come home! or else all will go wrong! | Schnell heim, sonst geht's nicht gut!

DAVID
(who has watched Walther with astonishment.)

A Master! Oho! You're bold!   Gleich Meister? Oho! viel Muth!

Scene Two. *Magdalene hurriedly pulls Eva away through the curtains. Walther throws himself, excited and brooding, into a high-backed ecclesiastical chair, which two of the prentices have previously moved from the wall towards the middle of the stage. More prentices enter bringing benches and placing them in position, preparing everything for the Mastersingers.*

1ST PRENTICE

David! Come on.   David, was stehst?

2ND PRENTICE

Lend a hand!   Greif' an's Werk!

3RD PRENTICE

Come and help us with the stand.   Hilf uns richten das Gemerk!

DAVID

I'm always the one who is working;   Zu eifrigst war ich vor euch allen;
Work now yourselves, and leave me in   schafft nun für euch; hab' ander
   quiet.   Gefallen!

2NS PRENTICE

Oho! such airs!   Was der sich dünkt!

3RD PRENTICE

How proud and haughty!   Der Lehrling' Muster!

1ST PRENTICE

Because he gets strapped when he's naughty!   Das macht, weil sein Meister ein Schuster.

3RD PRENTICE

He sits and cobbles with a feather!   Beim Leisten sitzt er mit der Feder.

2ND PRENTICE

Makes poems with thread and string!   Beim Dichten mit Draht und Pfriem'.

1ST PRENTICE

He writes his verses on greasy leather.   Sein' Verse schreibt er auf rohes Leder.

3RD PRENTICE
(with an appropriate gesture)

He knows, too, how it can sting!   Das, dächt' ich, gerbten wir ihm!

(They pursue their work at the back, laughing.)

DAVID
(watching the pensive knight for a moment, he calls loudly)

Now begin!   "Fanget an!"

WALTHER
(looking up, surprised)

What's this?   Was soll's?

DAVID
(louder)

Now begin! – So cries the Marker: "Fanget an!" – So ruft der "Merker";
Then you start singing! Don't you know   nun sollt ihr singen: – wisst ihr das nicht?
   that?

WALTHER

Who is the Marker?   Wer ist der Merker?

DAVID

Don't you know that?   Wisst ihr das nicht?
Have you not been at a singing trial?   War't ihr noch nie bei 'nem Sing-Gericht?

WALTHER

Not yet, where the judges were craftsmen.　　Noch nie, wo die Richter Handwerker!

DAVID

Are you a "Poet"?　　Seid ihr ein "Dichter"?

WALTHER

Would I were!　　Wär' ich's doch!

DAVID

Are you a "Singer"?　　Seid ihr ein "Singer"?

WALTHER

Would I knew!　　Wüsst ich's noch!

DAVID

But "Student" surely, or "Scholar" you've been?　　Doch "Schulfreund" war't ihr, und "Schüler" zuvor?

WALTHER

But all these words sound strange to me!　　Das klingt mir Alles fremd vor'm Ohr.

DAVID

And yet you would be a Mastersinger?　　Und so grad'hin wollt ihr Meister werden?

WALTHER

You think I am inviting disaster?　　Wie machte das so grosse Beschwerden?

DAVID

O Lene! Lene!　　O Lene! Lene!

WALTHER

What do you mean?　　Wie ihr doch thut!

DAVID

O Magdalene!　　O Magdalene!

WALTHER

Counsel me well!　　Rathet mir gut!

DAVID

My lord! The Mastersinger's way
Cannot be found in just one day.
In Nuremberg the finest Master
　Is now the great Hans Sachs:
For a full year he has taught me,
　So that a scholar I wax.
Shoemaker's craft and poet's art
Both daily I learn by heart;
First all the leather smooth I hammer,
Then all the vowels and consonants
　stammer;
Next must the thread be stiff with wax,
Then I must learn, it rhymes with Sachs.
　　With thread and needle
　　Make stitches neat,
　　And then I learn,
　　About time and beat,
　　With leather and last,
　　The slow, the fast,
　　The hard, the light,
　　Gloomy or bright,
　　The scissors, the snippings,
　　And word-clippings,
　　The pauses and corns,
　　The flowers and thorns,
I learned all this with care and pains;
To what now think you that it attains?

[10] Mein Herr! der Singer Meister-Schlag
gewinnt sich nicht in einem Tag.
In Nürnberg der grösste Meister,
　mich lehrt die Kunst Hans Sachs;
schon voll ein Jahr mich unterweis't er,
[11]　dass ich als Schüler wachs'.
Schuhmacherei und Poeterei,
die lern' ich da all einerlei:
hab' ich das Leder glatt geschlagen,
lern' ich Vocal und Consonanz sagen;
wichst' ich den Draht gar fein und steif,
was sich da reimt, ich wohl begreif';
　　den Pfriemen schwingend,
　　im Stich die Ahl',
　　was stumpf, was klingend,
　　was Mass und Zahl, –
　　den Leisten im Schurz –
　　was lang, was kurz,
　　was hart, was lind,
　　hell oder blind,
　　was Waisen, was Mylben,
　　was Kleb-Sylben,
　　was Pausen, was Körner,
　　Blumen und Dörner,
das Alles lernt' ich mit Sorg' und Acht:
wie weit nun, meint ihr, dass ich's gebracht?

Surely a pair of well-made shoes?

Wohl zu 'nem Paar recht guter Schuh'?

DAVID

Ah, there is time enough for that!
A "Bar" of many stanzas is made:
And the rules alone would break your head,
And rightly stitched
And truly pitched
Must word to tone be mated,
Well soled and heeled and fitted!
And then there comes the After-song,
One not too short and not too long;
And in it no rhyme may sound
That in the stanza is found.
When all this you've read, marked and learned,
You have still the name of Master not earned.

Ja, dahin hat's noch lange Ruh'!
Ein "Bar" hat manch' Gesätz' und Gebänd';
wer da gleich die rechte Regel fänd',
die richt'ge Nacht,
und den rechten Draht,
mit gutgefügten "Stollen",
den Bar recht zu versohlen.
Und dann erst kommt der "Abgesang";
dass der nicht kurz, und nicht zu lang,
und auch keinen Reim enthält,
der schon im Stollen gestellt. –
Wer Alles das merkt, weiss und kennt,
wird doch immer noch nicht "Meister" genennt.

WALTHER

Oh Heaven, teach me no cobbler's trade –
Rather tell me how a singer's made!

Hilf Gott! Will ich denn Schuster sein? –
In die Singkunst lieber führ' mich ein.

DAVID

Ah, that would already a singer I were!

Ja, hätt' ich's nur selbst erst zum "Singer" gebracht!

Who knows what time it needs and care!
The Masters' tones and measures [12]
Are many in name and kind;
The strong ones and the gentle
Who at once their names can find?
Then shortened, long, and overlong tones,
The scarlet ink, the paper mode;

Wer glaubt wohl, was das für Mühe macht?
Der Meister Tön' und Weisen,
gar viel an Nam' und Zahl,
die starken und die leisen,
wer die wüsste allzumal!
Der "kurze", "lang" und "überlang" Ton,
die "Schreibpapier", – "Schwarz-Dinten" – Weis';

The crimson, blue and green tones;
The strawberry, hawthorn, fennel mode;

der "rothe", "blau'" und "grüne" Ton,
die "Hageblüh", – "Strohhalm", – "Fengel" – Weis';

The tender, the winning, the rosy tone;

der "zarte", der "süsse", der "Rosen" – Ton;

The passing passion, the forgotten tone;
The rosemary, wall-flower mode;
The rainbow mode and the nightingale mode;
The English tin, the cinnamon mode,

der "kurzen Liebe", der "vergess'ne" Ton;
die "Rosmarin", – "Gelbveiglein" – Weis',
die "Regenbogen", – die "Nachtigall' – Weiss',
die "englische Zinn", – die "Zimmtröhren" – Weis',

Fresh pomegranates, and linden tree mode;

"frisch' Pomeranzen", – "grün Lindenblüh" – Weiss',

The frog, the calf, the linnet mode;

die "Frösch", – die "Kälber", – die "Stieglitz" – Weis',

The lonely gormandizer mode,
The sky-lark, the snail, the barking tone;

die "abgeschiedene Vielfrass" – Weis';
der "Lerchen", – der "Schnecken", – der "Beller" – Ton,

And the honey-flower, the marjoram,

die "Melissenblümlein", – die "Meiran" – Weis',

The lion skin, true pelican mode,
The bright glittering thread mode . . .

"Gelblöwenhaut", – "treu Pelikan" – Weis',
die "buttglänzende Draht" – Weis' . . .

WALTHER

Heaven help me! What endless medleys of tones!

Hilf Himmel! Welch endlos' Töne-Geleis'!

DAVID

These are but the titles; now comes the singing,
Just as the Masters have decreed;

Das sind nur die Namen: nun lernt sie singen,
recht wie die Meister sie gestellt!

Each word and tone most clearly ringing,
The voice must mount or fall at need:
Don't start too high or low in pitch,
But where the voice all notes can reach,
For the breath take care control to keep,
For fear of ending with a squeak!
When a word you begin, you must not
  groan
And in ending the voice must not moan.

Don't alter the turns or coloratur;
Each grace-note take from the Master's
  store.
For if you go wrong, stumble or trip,
Or lose yourself, or make but a slip: –
  Though all things else you sing
    correctly,
  For this you are still rejected.
Despite much effort, toil and care,
I never yet have come so far:
Each hopeful attempt new failure brings,
The knee-strap-stroke-mode my Master
  then sings.
And when to my Lene I cannot turn,
I sing alone the bread and water strain.
    Then learn this lesson well;
    Beware the Master spell!
Till singer and poet he has been,

No-one the Master's crown can win.

Jed' Wort und Ton muss klärlich klingen,
wo steigt die Stimm', und wo sie fällt.
Fangt nicht zu hoch, zu tief nicht an,
als es die Stimm' erreichen kann;
mit dem Athem spart, dass er nicht knappt;
und gar am End' ihr überschnappt.
Vor dem Wort mit der Stimme ja nicht
  summt,
nach dem Wort mit dem Mund auch nicht
  brummt,
nich ändert an "Blum" und "Coloratur",
jed' Zierrath fest nach des Meister's Spur;

verwechselt ihr, würdet gar irr,
verlör't ihr euch, und kämt in's Gewirr: –
  wär' sonst euch Alles gelungen,

    da hättet ihr gar "versungen!" –
Trotz grossem Fleiss und Emsigkeit
ich selbst noch bracht' es nie so weit.
So oft ich's versuch' und's nicht gelingt,
die "Knieriem-Schlag-Weis" der Meister
  mir singt:
wenn dann Jungfer Lene nicht Hülfe weiss,
sing' ich die "eitel Brod-und-Wasser-Weis'!"
    Nehmt euch ein Beispiel dran,
    und lasst von dem Meister-Wahn!
Denn "Singer" und "Dichter" müsst ihr
  sein,
[3] eh' ihr zum "Meister" kehret ein.

WALTHER

What makes a poet?   Wer ist nun Dichter?

PRENTICES
(while they are working)

David! Come here!   David! kommst' her?

DAVID

Wait awhile, wait! –   Wartet nur, gleich!

(quickly turning back to Walther)

A poet you ask?   Wer "Dichter" wär'?
When as a singer you've graduated   Habt ihr zum "Singer" euch auf-
  geschwungen
And the Master tones have sung as I've   und der Meister Töne richtig gesungen,
  stated,
If you yourself in true accord   füget ihr selbst nun Reim und Wort',
Find and unite both rhyme and word   dass sie genau an Stell' und Ort
So that they fit some Master tone: passten zu einem Meister-Ton,
Then you've made the poet's prize your   [3] dann trüg't ihr den Dichterpreis davon.
  own.

PRENTICES

Hey! David! Must we then call your   He, David! Soll man's dem Meister klagen?
  master?
Will you never have done with your   Wirst dich bald des Schwatzens
  chatter?   entschlagen?

DAVID

Oho! I see, if I leave you for long   Oho! – Ja wohl! Denn helf' ich euch nicht,
Everything you do goes completely wrong!   ohne mich wird Alles doch falsch gericht'!

(He is about to go to them.)

WALTHER
(holding him back)

But tell me; who as "Master" you name?   Nur dies noch: wer wird "Meister" gennant?

51

DAVID
(turning quickly back)

My lord, a Master we thus proclaim: –	Damit, Herr Ritter, ist's so bewandt: –
The poet who by faithful striving	der Dichter, der aus eig'nem Fleisse
To words and rhymes he himself has found,	zu Wort' und Reimen, die er erfand,
A melody adds of his own contriving.	aus Tönen auch fügt eine neue Weise:
He will as "Mastersinger" be crowned.	der wird als "Meistersinger" erkannt.

WALTHER
(quickly)

One path alone then to Master's name!	So bleibt mir nichts als der Meisterlohn!
That by Heaven [2]	Soll ich hier singen,
Grace may be given	kann's nur gelingen,
Rightly to fashion a master strain.	find' ich zum Versuch den eig'nen Ton.

DAVID
(who has turned to the prentices)
[9]

What's this that you've done? When I'm not at hand,	Was macht ihr denn da? – ja, fehl' ich beim Werk,
You all go wrong with the chair and the stand.	verkehrt nur richtet ihr Stuhl und Gemerk! –
Is it not song-school? That you know!	Ist denn heut' "Singschul'"? – dass ihr's wisst,
The chair must be here! It's trials today.	das kleine Gemerk! – nur "Freiung" ist!

The prentices, who have put up a large screen of curtains in the middle of the stage, take it down under David's directions and replace it with a smaller dais; on this they place a chair, a small desk and a large black-board with a piece of chalk attached by a string; black curtains are pulled around it, first at the back and sides, and then at the front.

PRENTICES
(as they work)

Such a scholar as David we've never yet seen;	Aller End' ist doch David der Allergescheit'st!
Glory and honour he surely must win:	Nach hohen Ehren gewiss er geizt:
Perhaps he may	's ist Freiung heut;
Be freed today;	gar sicher er freit,
The finest of singers he long has been.	als vornehmer "Singer" schon er sich spreizt!
The strap-leather mode has made him smart,	Die "Schlag"-reime fest er inne hat,
The hunger tune he knows by heart!	"Arm-Hunger"-Weise singt er glatt;
And the hearty-kick mode he carefully learns,	die "harte-Tritt"-Weis' doch kennt er am best',
His Master employs them all by turns.	die trat ihm sein Meister hart und fest!

(They laugh.)

DAVID

Yes, laugh away! But not at me.	Ja, lacht nur zu! Heut' bin ich's nicht;
Another candidate you will see;	ein Andrer stellt sich zum Gericht:
Who's not a scholar, nor a singer,	der war nicht "Schüler", ist nicht "Singer",
As poet too, he's a beginner;	den "Dichter", sagt er, überspring' er;
A gallant knight,	denn er ist Junker,
He, in single flight	und mit einem Sprung er
Now hopes without ruin or disaster	denkt ohne weit're Beschwerden,
Today to be Master.	heut' hier "Meister" zu werden. –
So quickly make ready	D'rum richtet nur fein
The Marker's place!	Das Gemerk dem ein!
Here now! – There now! The black slate on the wall,	Dorthin! – Hierher! Die Tafel an die Wand,
All ready for the Marker's hand.	so dass sie recht dem Merker zur Hand!

(turning to Walther)

Ah, yes, the Marker! Do you grow pale?	Ja, ja! – dem "Merker"! – Wird euch wohl bang?
Before him many candidates fail.	Vor ihm schon mancher Werber versang.
Seven faults the Marker lets by,	Sieben Fehler giebt er euch vor,

With chalk they are marked on the slate:	die merkt er mit Kreide dort an;
If more than seven faults he should spy,	wer über sieben Fehler verlor,
Then the singer has met his fate!	hat versungen und ganz verthan!
So you must take care,	Nun nehmt euch in Acht!
The Marker's there.	Der Merker wacht,
Good luck to Mastersinging!	Glück auf zum Meistersingen!
May you your garland be winning!	Mögt' ihr euch das Kränzlein erschwingen!
The silken garland of flowers bright,	Das Blumenkränzlein aus Seiden fein,
Will that by good fortune be yours, Sir Knight?	wird das dem Herrn Ritter beschieden sein?

PRENTICES

(Having completed the marker's dais, they take hands and dance around it.)

The silken garland of flowers bright,	"Das Blumenkränzlein aus Seiden fein,
Will that by good fortune be yours, Sir Knight?	wird das dem Herrn Ritter beschieden sein?"

(The prentices separate in alarm as the sacristy opens and Pogner and Beckmesser enter; they retire to the back.)

Scene Three. *The arrangement of the stage is now completed; on the right cushioned benches are placed in a curve facing the centre. At the end of the benches, in the middle of the stage, is the Marker's dais. On the left stands the high-backed chair (the "Singer's chair"). At the back, in front of the great curtain, a long, low bench for the pupils. Walther, angered by the jibes of the boys, has seated himself on the front bench. Pogner comes from the sacristy in conversation with Beckmesser as the other Masters gradually assemble. The Prentices, seeing the Masters enter, disperse and wait respectfully by the back bench; only David stands by the entrance to the sacristy.*

10 **POGNER**
(to Beckmesser) [14]

Be well assured of my good favour;	Seid meiner Treue wohl versehen;
What I have planned will serve you well:	was ich bestimmt, ist euch zu nutz:
Success will go with your endeavour;	im Wettgesang müsst ihr bestehen;
Who wields like you the Master's spell?	wer böte euch als Meister Trutz?

BECKMESSER

But won't you make this one concession,	Doch wollt ihr von dem Punkt nicht weichen,
For I confess I'm doubtful still:	der mich – ich sag's – bedenklich macht;
If Eva's wish can choose her lover,	kann Evchens Wunsch den Werber streichen,
What good is all my Master skill?	was nützt mir meine Meister-Pracht?

POGNER

And yet I feel that first of all you	Ei sagt! Ich mein', vor allen Dingen
Should try to learn how well you stand;	sollt' euch an dem gelegen sein?
For if her heart you fail in winning,	Könnt ihr der Tochter Wunsch nicht zwingen
How then can you desire her hand?	wie möchtet ihr wohl um sie frei'n?

BECKMESSER

Ah yes! Quite true! I therefore pray you	Ei ja! Gar wohl! D'rum eben bitt' ich,
That to the child you speak for me.	dass bei dem Kind ihr für mich sprecht,
Say I am kind and very gentle,	wie ich geworben zart und sittig,
And that Beckmesser you approve.	und wie Beckmesser grad euch recht.

POGNER

With right good will.	Das thu' ich gern.

BECKMESSER
(aside)

He won't give way.	Er lässt nicht nach!
I view the future with dismay!	Wie wehrt' ich da 'nem Ungemach?

WALTHER
(rising to meet Pogner, he bows)

Your pardon Master!   Gestattet, Meister!

POGNER

What, Sir Walther?   Wie! mein Junker!
You seek me in the singing school?   Ihr sucht mich in der Singschul' hie?

(Pogner and Walther exchange greetings.)

BECKMESSER
(still aside)

If women had wits! But high sounding folly   Verstünden's die Frau'n! Doch schlechtes Geflunker

Pleases them more than poetry's charms!   Gilt ihnen mehr als all' Poesie.

(He walks up and down at the back in vexation.)

WALTHER

That here you find me is only right,   [14]   Hie eben bin ich am rechten Ort.
For, you must know I left my home   Gesteh' ich's frei, vom Lande fort
   And came to Nuremberg town,   Was mich nach Nürnberg trieb,
   For love of art alone.   war nur zur Kunst die Lieb'.
Until today I failed to say it,   Vergass ich's gestern euch zu sagen,
Now must I openly proclaim it;   heut' mass ich's laut zu künden wagen:
A Mastersinger I would be!   ein Meistersinger möcht' ich sein.
Pray, of your guild now make me free!   Schliesst, Meister, in die Zunft mich ein!

(Enter Kunz Vogelgesang and Conrad Nachtigall.)

POGNER
(turning happily to the newcomers)

Kunz Vogelgesang! Friend Nachtigall!   Kunz Vogelgesang! Freund Nachtigall!
Here is a most unusual case!   Hört doch, welch' ganz besonderer Fall!
This noble knight, to me well known,   Der Ritter hier, mir wohlbekannt,
To our Master art his thought would   hat der Meisterkunst sich zugewandt.
   turn.

(Introductions and greetings: others Mastersingers come forward.)

BECKMESSER
(coming again to the front, aside)

Once more I will ask him, and if he   Noch such' ich's zu wenden: doch sollt's
   refuse me,   nicht gelingen,
With song I will charm the maiden to   versuch' ich des Mädchens Herz zu ersingen;
   choose
   me.
I'll sing at night for her ears alone: in stiller Nacht, von ihr nur gehört,
Perhaps by singing she may be won.   erfahr' ich, ob auf mein Lied sie schwört.
(seeing Walther)

Who is this man?   Wer ist der Mensch?

POGNER
(continuing very warmly to Walther)

Warm is my heart!   Glaubt, wie mich's freut!
The days of old are born anew.   Die alte Zeit dünkt mich erneu't.

BECKMESSER
(still to himself)

He displeases me!   Er gefällt mir nicht!

POGNER
(to Walther)

What you desire,   Was ihr begehrt,
If mine to grant, you can command.   soviel an mir, euch sei's gewährt.

BECKMESSER
(aside)

Why is he here? With his laughing looks!   Was will der hier? – Wie der Blick ihm lacht!

POGNER
(continuing)

Gladly I helped you your land to sell,	Half ich euch gern bei des Gut's Verkauf,
To our guild I welcome you now as well.	in die Zunft nun nehm' ich euch gleich
	gern auf.

BECKMESSER
(as before)

Holla Sixtus! Beware of him!	Holla! Sixtus! Auf den hab' Acht!

WALTHER
(to Pogner)

For all your goodness	Habt Dank der Güte
Most deeply I thank you,	aus tiefstem Gemüthe!
And dare I to hope then	Und darf ich denn hoffen,
The way is now open	steht heut' mir noch offen
For me the prize to claim	zu werben um den Preis,
Of Mastersinger's name?	dass ich Meistersinger heiss'?

BECKMESSER

Oho! So fast! Then the knight's on his	Oho! Fein sacht! Auf dem Kopf steht kein
mettle!	Kegel!

POGNER

Sir Walther, we must respect procedure.	Herr Ritter, dies geh' nun nach der Regel.
Today is Trial, but have no fear;	Doch heut' ist Freiung: ich schlag' euch vor;
I gain from the Masters a willing ear.	mir leihen die Meister ein willig Ohr.

(All the Masters have now arrived, Hans Sachs last.)

SACHS

God greet you, Masters!	Gott grüss' euch, Meister!

VOGELGESANG

Are we all here now?	Sind wir beisammen?

BECKMESSER

Yes, Sachs has arrived.	Der Sachs ist ja da!

NACHTIGALL

Then call the names out.	So ruft die Namen!

FRITZ KOTHNER
(He produces a list, takes his place apart, and calls out.)

Now to trial, as summoned hither,	[14] Zu einer Freiung und Zunftberathung
Masters in council are come together:	ging an die Meister ein' Einladung:
Of one and all	bei Nenn' und Nam',
The names I call,	ob jeder kam,
And, as the last elected Master,	ruf' ich nun auf, als letzt-entbot'ner,
I name myself and call Fritz Kothner.	der ich mich nenn' und bin Fritz Kothner.
Are you there, Veit Pogner?	Seid ihr da, Veit Pogner?

POGNER

Here at hand!	Hier zur Hand.
(sits)	

KOTHNER

Kunz Vogelgesang?	Kunz Vogelgesang?

VOGELGESANG

Here I stand.	Ein sich fand.
(sits)	

KOTHNER

Hermann Ortel?	Hermann Ortel?

ORTEL

Comes when he ought.   Immer am Ort.

(sits)

KOTHNER

Balthasar Zorn?   Balthasar Zorn?

ZORN

Here on the spot.   Bleibt niemals fort.

(sits)

KOTHNER

Conrad Nachtigall?   Konrad Nachtigall?

NACHTIGALL

True to his lay.   Treu seinem Schlag.

(sits)

KOTHNER

Augustin Moser?   Augustin Moser?

MOSER

Never away.   Nie fehlen mag.

(sits)

KOTHNER

Niklaus Vogel? – Well?   Niklaus Vogel? – Schweigt?

PRENTICE
(jumping up from his seat)

He's ill.   Ist krank.

KOTHNER

Good health to the Master!   Gut' Bess'rung dem Meister!

ALL THE MASTERS

Amen!   Walt's Gott!

PRENTICE

His thanks!   Schön Dank!

(He sits down again.)

KOTHNER

Hans Sachs?   Hans Sachs?

DAVID
(rising and pointing to Sachs)

He's there now!   Da steht er!

SACHS
(threateningly to David)

How dare you stand?   Juckt dich das Fell? –
Forgive, Masters, here if you please.   Verzeiht Meister! – Sachs ist zur Stell'.

(sits)

KOTHNER

Sixtus Beckmesser?   Sixtus Beckmesser?

BECKMESSER

Always with Sachs,   Immer bei Sachs,
Thus the rhyme I learn to "bloom and wax"!   dass den Reim ich lern' von "blüh' und wachs'".

(sits next to Sachs, who laughs)

KOTHNER

Ulrich Eisslinger?   Ulrich Eisslinger?

EISSLINGER

Here!   Hier!
(*sits*)

KOTHNER

Hans Foltz?   Hans Foltz?

FOLTZ

Here, too.   Bin da.
(*sits*)

KOTHNER

Hans Schwarz?   Hans Schwarz?

SCHWARZ

At last: Praise God!   Zuletzt: Gott wollt's!
(*sits*)

KOTHNER

The council, I declare, is met.   Zur Sitzung gut und voll die Zahl.
Shall we make choice of a Marker now?   Beliebt's, wir schreiten zur Merkerwahl?

VOGELSANG

The festival first.   Wohl eh'r nach dem Fest.

BECKMESSER
(*to Kothner*)

So pressing, sirs?   Pressirt's den Herrn!
My place to you gladly I yield.   Mein Stell' und Amt lass' ich ihm gern.

POGNER

Not so; my Masters, let that alone,   Nicht doch, ihr Meister! Lasst das jetzt fort.
A weighty matter I would make known.   Für wicht'gen Antrag bitt' ich um's Wort.

(*The Masters rise, nod to Kothner, and reseat themselves.*)

KOTHNER

Now tell us, Master speak!   Das habt ihr, Meister! Sprecht!

POGNER

Then hear and attend ye well!   Nun hört, und versteht mich recht!
The feast of John, Midsummer day,   [15] Das schöne Fest, Johannis-Tag,
    Ye know we keep tomorrow.   ihr wisst, begeh'n wir morgen:
In meadows green, by hedges gay,   auf grüner Au', am Blumenhag,
With song and dance among the hay,   bei Spiel und Tanz im Lustgelag,
    With heart so full of gladness,   an froher Brust geborgen,
Forgetting all his sadness,   vergessen seiner Sorgen,
Let each rejoice as best he may.   ein Jeder freut sich, wie er mag.
The Singing School will raise on high   Die Singschul' ernst im Kirchenchor
    A hymn of praise and glory,   die Meister selbst vertauschen;
With joyous sounds and hearts aglow   mit Kling und Klang hinaus zum Thor,
Into the meadows we will go,   auf off'ne Wiese ziehn sie vor,
    Amid the festive thronging   bei hellen Festes Rauschen;
The folk shall hear resounding   das Volk sie lassen lauschen
The songs that Mastersingers know.   dem Frei-Gesang mit Laien-Ohr.
When gifts are won in strife of song   Zu einem Werb' – und Wett-Gesang
    That blithely swells and rises,   gestellt sind Siegespreise,
Then acclamations loud and long   und beide rühmt man weit und lang,
    Will greet both songs and prizes.   die Gabe wie die Weise.
As God made me a wealthy man;   Nun schuf mich Gott zum reichen Mann;
And each one gives as best he can,   und giebt ein Jeder, wie er kann,
    I sought among my treasure   so musst' ich fleissig sinnen,
A gift beyond all measure,   was ich gäb' zu gewinnen,
Lest I to shame be brought;   dass ich nicht käm' zu Schand':
I found then what I sought.   so höret, was ich fand. –

In all my journeys far and wide,   In deutschen Landen viel gereis't,
    I oft was angered greatly,   hat oft es mich verdrossen,

Finding we burghers were decried
  As selfish and unfriendly.
In castle and in humble hut,
The evil slander ended not,
  That only treasure and gold
  Our burghers' dreams can hold!
Though in our country's spacious bounds
  The arts we alone have tended,
  For this we are little commended.
But how our deeds do honour us all,
  And how in steadfast mood,
  We cherish the fair and good,
The power of art and all its worth   [14]
To that I would here bear witness on earth:
  This gift, then, I choose as prize:
  May ye Masters think it wise!
To him whose song among the rest,   [15, 14]
In contest here you judge the best,
  On John the Baptist's Day,
  Let him be who he may,
  Him give I, a Mastersinger
  Of Nuremberg, Veit Pogner,
With all I possess, and all I own
  Eva, my only child, as bride.

dass man den Bürger wenig preis't,
  ihn karg nennt und verschlossen:
an Höfen, wie an nied'rer Statt,
des bitt'ren Tadels ward ich satt,
  dass nur auf Schacher und Geld
  sein Merk' der Bürger stellt'.
Dass wir im weiten deutschen Reich
  die Kunst einzig noch pflegen,
  d'ran dünkt' ihnen wenig gelegen:
doch wie uns das zur Ehre gereich',
  und dass mit hohem Muth
  wir schätzen, was schön und gut,
was werth die Kunst, und was sie gilt,
das ward ich der Welt zu zeigen gewillt.
  D'rum hört, Meister, die Gab',
  die als Preis bestimmt ich hab':
dem Singer, der im Kunst-Gesang
vor allem Volk den Preis errang
  am Sankt Johannistag,
  sei er, wer er auch mag,
  dem geb' ich, ein Kunst-gewog'ner,
  von Nürenberg Veit Pogner,
mit all' meinem Gut, wie's geh' und steh',
  Eva, mein einzig Kind, zur Eh'.

MASTERSINGERS
(rising and speaking to each other with great animation)

His words are brave, like word, like man!
He speaks as only Nurembergers can!
We'll sing your praises far and wide,
Our worthy burgher Pogner Veit!

Das nenn' ich ein Wort! Ein Wort, ein Mann!
Da sieht man, was ein Nürnberger kann!
D'rob preis't man euch noch weit und breit,
den wack'ren Bürger Pogner Veit!

PRENTICES
(jumping up merrily)

All our days, we will raise
  Pogner's praise!

Alle Zeit, weit und breit:
  Pogner Veit!

VOGELGESANG

Who would not now unwedded be?

Wer möchte da nicht ledig sein!

SACHS

There's some would give their wives with glee!

Sein Weib gäb' gern wohl mancher d'rein!

KOTHNER
(to Beckmesser)

Now single man!
Do what you can!

Auf ledig Mann!
Jetzt macht euch 'ran!

(The Masters and prentices gradually take their seats again.)

POGNER

Now Masters, hear what I decree!
A lifeless gift I will not give,
The maid herself will help to judge.
The prize shall go as wills the guild;
But maidens' hearts may not be willed;
  And whom the Masters choose,
  The bride may still refuse.

Nun hört noch, wie ich's ernstlich mein'!
Ein' leblos' Gabe stell' ich nicht:
ein Mägdlein sitzt mit zu Gericht.
Den Preis erkennt die Meister-Zunft;
doch gilt's der Eh', so will's Vernunft,
  dass ob der Meister Rath
  die Braut den Ausschlag hat.

BECKMESSER
(to Pogner)

You think that wise?

Dünkt euch das klug?

KOTHNER
(loudly)

       I understand,
You place us in the maiden's hand?

       Versteh' ich gut,
ihr gebt uns in des Mägdlein's Huth?

BECKMESSER

There's danger there!	Gefährlich das!

KOTHNER

Must we agree?	Stimmt es nicht bei,
Who then could call the Masters'	wie wäre dann der Meister Urtheil frei?
judgement free?	

BECKMESSER

Whom she loves let her heart proclaim,	Lasst's gleich wählen nach Herzens Ziel,
And leave the Mastersong out of the game!	und lasst den Meistergesang aus dem Spiel!

POGNER

Not so! And why? Let me explain!	Nicht so! Wie doch? Versteht mich recht!
If your judgement elects a man	Wem ihr Meister den Preis zusprecht,
Who fails to gain her favour,	die Maid kann dem verwehren:
Unwedded she lives then forever.	doch nie einen Andren begehren:
A Mastersinger must he be:	[1a] ein Meistersinger muss er sein;
He who is crowned and none but he!	nur wen ihr krönt, den soll sie frei'n.

HOUSTON

SACHS

Aha!	Verzeiht!
With that I think you've gone too far.	Vielleicht schon ginget ihr zu weit.
A maiden's love and Master's aim	Ein Mädchenherz und Meisterkunst
Will hardly burn with equal flame;	erglüh'n nicht stets von gleicher Brunst;
A woman's thought, the people's mind,	der Frauen Sinn, gar unbelehrt,
They are to me alike in kind.	dünkt mich dem Sinn des Volks gleich werth.
If you would clearly show your neighbours	Wollt ihr nun vor dem Volke zeigen,
How well you love your art,	wie hoch die Kunst ihr ehrt;
And let Eva choose the man she favours,	und lasst ihr dem Kind die Wahl zu eigen,
Yet not have your verdict barred,	wollt nicht, dass dem Spruch es wehrt':
Then let the folk the judges be,	so lasst das Volk auch Richter sein;
With the maid, I'm certain, they will agree!	mit dem Kinde sicher stimmt's überein.

MASTERINGERS
(uneasily)

Oho! Aye, that would be good!	Oho! Das Volk? Ja, das wäre schön!
Farewell then, Art and Masterhood!	Ade dann Kunst und Meistertön!

KOTHNER

Nay, Sachs! Indeed that's plainly absurd!	Nein, Sachs! Gewiss, das hat keinen Sinn!
Why give the folk the final word?	Gäb't ihr dem Volk die Regeln hin?

SACHS

But hear me out! Why argue so?	Vernehmt mich recht! Wie ihr doch thut
Confess, the rules right well I know;	Gesteht, ich kenn' die Regeln gut;
And that those rules should suffer no slight,	und dass die Zunft die Regeln bewahr',
Has been my endeavour day and night.	bemüh' ich mich selbst schon manches Jahr.
But once every year it might be better,	Doch einmal im Jahre fänd' ich's weise,
To put those rules themselves to a test,	dass man die Regeln selbst probir',
To find out if following custom forever	ob in der Gewohnheit trägem G'leise
Their force and life be still at their best!	ihr Kraft und Leben sich nicht verlier':
And if you would be sure	[14] und ob ihr der Natur
You follow Nature's law,	noch seid auf rechter Spur,
Ask folk unskilled	das sagt euch nur,
Who don't know of the rules of our Guild.	wer nichts weiss von der Tabulatur.

(The prentices jump up and rub their hands.)

BECKMESSER

Hey! See how the boys make merry!	Hei! wie sich die Buben freuen!

SACHS
(eagerly continuing)

I'm sure you will not regret it,	D'rum mocht's euch nie gereuen,
If only on each Midsummer day,	dass jährlich am Sankt Johannisfest,
Turning aside from custom's way,	statt dass das Volk man kommen lässt,

You leave your realm of mist and cloud
And turn yourselves towards the crowd.
    To give the people some pleasure,
    We know our aim to be;
    We'd lay before them the matter,
    And ask them if they agree.
Thus folk and art both bloom and grow.

It might well be, Hans Sachs thinks so!

herab aus hoher Meister-Wolk'
ihr selbst euch wendet zu dem Volk'.
    Dem Volke wollt ihr behagen;
    nun dächt ich, läg' es nah',
    ihr liesst es selbst euch auch sagen,
    ob das ihm zur Lust geschah.
Dass Volk und Kunst gleich blüh' und wachs',

bestellt ihr so, mein' ich, Hans Sachs.

VOGELGESANG

You mean right well!

[1b] Ihr meint's wohl recht!

KOTHNER

And yet you're wrong.

Doch steh's drum faul.

NACHTIGALL

If mobs may speak I hold my tongue!

Wenn spricht das Volk, halt' ich das Maul.

KOTHNER

But shame will fall upon our art,
If in our work the crowd takes part.

Der Kunst droht allweil' Fall und Schmach,
läuft sie der Gunst des Volkes nach.

BECKMESSER

Shame has he brought who talks so loud:
Writing doggerel rhymes for the crowd.

D'rin bracht' er's weit, der hier so dreist
Gassenhauer dichtet er meist.

POGNER

Friend Sachs! What I mean is quite new,
Too much at one time we should rue!
I ask then, if all Masters allow
Prize and reasons as I state them now.

Freund Sachs, was ich mein', ist schon neu:
zuviel auf einmal brächte Reu'! –
So frag' ich, ob den Meistern gefällt
Gab' und Regel, wie ich's gestellt?

(The Masters rise in assent.)
[14, 15]

14 SACHS

Let the maiden choose and I agree.

Mir genügt der Jungfer Ausschlag-Stimm'.

BECKMESSER
(to himself)

This shoemaker enrages me!

Der Schuster weckt doch stets mir Grimm!

KOTHNER

Who comes as a suitor here?
Now bachelors, all draw near!

Wer schreibt sich als Werber ein?
Ein Jung-Gesell muss es sein.

BECKMESSER

Perhaps too a widower? Just ask Sachs!

Vielleicht auch ein Wittwer? Fragt nur den Sachs!

SACHS

Not so, dear Marker! A younger man

Than I or you must the suitor be,
If Eva's choice with ours agree.

Nicht doch, Herr Merker! Aus jüng'rem Wachs

als ich und ihr muss der Freier sein,
soll Evchen ihm den Preis verleih'n.

BECKMESSER

Than you or I? – Ill-mannered boor!

Als wie auch ich? – Grober Gesell!

KOTHNER

Who comes a-wooing? Why be afraid!
Is anyone here who wishes to wed?

Begehrt wer Freiung, der komm' zur Stell'!
Ist Jemand gemeld't, der Freiung begehrt?

POGNER

Now Masters, to duty let us turn!
    And hear from me the news,
    That as a Master should,

Wohl, Meister! Zur Tagesordnung kehrt!
    Und nehmt von mir Bericht,
    wie ich auf Meister-Pflicht

A youthful knight I present you,
Who wills that we elect him
And here as Master make him free.
The knight von Stolzing, here you see!

einen jungen Ritter empfehle,
der wünscht, dass man ihn wähle,
und heut' als Meistersinger frei'. –
Mein Junker von Stolzing, kommt herbei!

(*Walther comes forward and bows.*) [16a]

BECKMESSER
(*aside*)

Just as I thought! Is that the plan, Veit?

Dacht' mir's doch! Geht's da hinaus, Veit?

(*aloud*)

Masters, perhaps the time is too late!

Meister, ich mein', zu spät ist's der Zeit.

MASTERSINGERS

The case is new. – A knight, indeed.
Should we be glad? – Is there danger here?
None the less it must have great weight
That Pogner for him speaks.

Der Fall ist neu. – Ein Ritter gar?
Soll man sich freu'n? – Oder wär' Gefahr?
Immerhin hat's ein gross' Gewicht,
dass Meister Pogner für ihn spricht.

KOTHNER

Yet, if the knight is to join our guild,
He first must be tried and duly passed.

Soll uns der Junker willkommen sein,
zuvor muss er wohl vernommen sein.

POGNER

Mistake me not! Friend though he be,
By rules alone you must your verdict agree.
Put, Master, the questions.

Vernehmt ihn gut! Wünsch' ich ihm Glück,
nicht bleib' ich doch hinter der Regel zurück.
Thut, Meister, die Fragen!

KOTHNER

Then first let the knight now tell us:
Are his birth and standing approved?

So mög' uns der Junker sagen:
ist er frei und ehrlich geboren?

POGNER

That question I will answer,
For I myself his bond will be
That he is nobly born and free:
The knight von Stolzing from Frankenland,
By name and letters to me well known,
As last descendant of his line,
He lately left his home and lands,
And came to Nuremberg here
To join our burghers' guild.

Die Frage gebt verloren,
da ich euch selbst dess' Bürge stch',
dass er aus frei und edler Eh':
von Stolzing Walther aus Frankenland,
nach Brief' und Urkund' mir wohlbekannt.
Als seines Stammes letzter Spross,
verliess er neulich Hof und Schloss,
und zog nach Nürnberg her,
dass er hier Bürger wär.

BECKMESSER
(*to his neighbour*)

Raw pompous upstart! Waste of time.

Neu Junker-Unkraut! Thut nicht gut.

NACHTIGALL
(*loudly*)

Friend Pogner's word is good enough.

Freund Pogner's Wort Genüge thut.

SACHS

The rule by the Masters was made of old,
That lord and peasant alike we hold:
Here nought is prized but art alone,
In those who seek the Master's crown.

Wie längst von den Meistern beschlossen ist,
ob Herr, ob Bauer, hier nichts beschliesst:
hier fragt sich's nach der Kunst allein,
wer will ein Meistersinger sein.

KOTHNER

Then his answer I claim:
His Master now let him name.

D'rum nun frag' ich zur Stell';
welch' Meister's seid ihr Gesell'?

WALTHER

By silent hearth one winter's day,
When locked in snow the castle lay,
How once the laughing spring did reign,
And swiftly now, must reign again,
An ancient book, to heart and brain,

Am stillen Herd in Winterszeit,
wenn Burg und Hof mir eingeschnei't,
wie einst der Lenz so lieblich lacht',
und wie er bald wohl neu erwacht',
ein altes Buch, vom Ahn' vermacht,

The blessed tidings brought me:
Sir Walther of the Vogelweid,
Was then the Master who taught me.

gab das mir oft zu lesen:
Herr Walther von der Vogelweid',
der ist mein Meister gewesen.

SACHS

A worthy master!

Ein guter Meister!

BECKMESSER

But long since dead:
From him I wonder what rules could be learned?

Doch lang' schon todt:
wie lehrt' ihn der wohl der Regel Gebot?

KOTHNER

In what school of art and singing
Did you receive your instruction?

Doch in welcher Schul' das Singen
mocht' euch zu lernen gelingen?

WALTHER

Then when the frost had passed away
And sunshine filled each summer's day;
What during winter's dreary spell
That ancient book had told so well,
    That song I heard o'er moor and fell,
Through field and forest ringing:
From birds' song on the Vogelweid,
    'Twas there I learned my singing.

Wann denn die Flur vom Frost befreit,
und wiederkehrt die Sommerszeit,
was einst in langer Winternacht
das alte Buch mir kund gemacht,
    das schallte laut in Waldespracht,
    das hört' ich hell erklingen:
im Wald dort auf der Vogelweid',
    da lernt' ich auch das Singen.

BECKMESSER

Oho! The finches and thrushes
Taught you our Master-singing?
What manner of teaching was theirs?

Oho! Von Finken und Meisen
Lerntet ihr Meister-Weisen?
Das mag denn wohl auch darnach sein!

VOGELGESANG

Two pleasing verses he has just sung.

Zwei art'ge Stollen fasst' er da ein.

BECKMESSER

You praise him, Master Vogelgesang,
Since from the birds he has learned all his song?

Ihr lobt ihn, Meister Vogelgesang?
Wohl weil er vom Vogel lernt' den Gesang?

KOTHNER
(aside to the Masters)

What say you, Masters, should we end here?
The knight already is wrong, I fear.

Was meint ihr, Meister? Frag' ich noch fort?
Mich dünkt, der Junker ist fehl am Ort.

SACHS

We must not judge too lightly
If art has led him rightly;
And good in sound and thought
Who minds by whom he was taught?

Das wird sich bäldlich zeigen
wenn rechte Kunst ihm eigen,
und gut er sie bewährt,
was gilt's, wer sie ihn gelehrt?

KOTHNER
(to Walther)

Are you prepared to show us all
If you have found a Mastersong
    With words and tune well mated,
    And by yourself created?

Seid ihr bereit, ob euch gerieth
mit neuer Find' ein Meisterlied,
    nach Dicht' und Weis' eu'r eigen,
    zur Stunde jetzt zu zeigen?

WALTHER

The secret deep
    Of winter's sleep,
Of woods in summer's glory,
The hidden word of book and bird,
Revealed in poet's story;
    The warlike clash
    When weapons flash,
    And music for
    A merry dance

Was Winternacht,
    was Waldes Pracht
was Buch und Hain mich wiesen;
was Dichter-Sanges Wundermacht
mir heimlich wollt' erschliessen;
    was Rosses Schritt
    beim Waffen-Ritt,
    was Reihen-Tanz
    bei heit'rem Schanz

Within my heart are ringing:
These now, to gain life's highest prize, [16b]
Must I proclaim in singing.
A song, my own, in word and tone,
I gladly now will bring you,
A Mastersong, if I am right,
My Masters, I will sing you.

mir sinnend gab zu lauschen:
gilt es des Lebens höchsten Preis
um Sang mir einzutauschen,
zu eig'nem Wort und eig'ner Weis'
will einig mir es fliessen,
als Meistersang, ob den ich weiss,
euch Meistern sich ergiessen.

BECKMESSER

What sense is in these whirling words?   Entnahmt ihr 'was der Worte Schwall?

VOGELGESANG

In truth, 'tis bold!   Ei nun, er wagt's!

NACHTIGALL

Strange is the case!   Merkwürd'ger Fall!

KOTHNER

Now Masters, with your leave
The Marker takes his place.
Does the Knight choose a holy theme?

Nun, Meister, wenn's gefällt,
werd' das Gemerk bestellt. –
Wählt der Herr einen heil'gen Stoff?

WALTHER

My holy sign,
The banner of love,
Waving o'er me, floats above!

Was heilig mir,
der Liebe Panier
schwing' und sing' ich, mir zu Hoff'.

KOTHNER

That call we worldly. Therefore now,
Master Beckmesser, take your place.

Das gilt uns weltlich. Drum allein,
Merker Beckmesser, schliesst euch ein!

BECKMESSER
(*rises and goes, as if unwillingly, to the Marker's dais.*)

A bitter task today I fear!
The chalk will be busy, well I know!
Sir Knight, take care,
Sixtus Beckmesser marketh here:
Here will he lurk
And silently do his rigorous work.
Seven faults he lets pass by,
With chalk they are marked on the slate:
But if more than seven faults he should spy, [16a]
Then, Sir Knight, you have met your fate.
His ears are keen;
But, lest your soul, if he were seen,
Should be distressed,
He leaves you at rest,
And hides himself away:
God grant you his grace today. [16a]

Ein sau'res Amt, und heut' zumal;
wohl giebt's mit der Kreide manche Qual. –
Herr Ritter, wisst:
Sixtus Beckmesser Merker ist;
hier im Gemerk
verrichtet er still sein strenges Werk.
Sieben Fehler giebt er euch vor,
die merkt er mit Kreide dort an:
wenn er über sieben Fehler verlor,
dann versang der Herr Rittersmann. –
Gar fein er hört;
doch dass er euch den Muth nicht stört,
säh't ich ihm zu,
so giebt er euch Ruh,
und schliesst sich gar hier ein, –
lässt Gott euch befohlen sein.

He has seated himself in the box and with the last words stretches his head out with a mocking, friendly nod, and draws the curtains (opened for him by a prentice) so that he disappears from view.

KOTHNER
(*taking down the "Leges Tabulaturae" which the prentices have hung on the wall*)

To make your footsteps safe and sure,
These rules come from the Tabulatur.

Was euch zum Liede Richt' und Schnur,
vernehmt nun aus der Tabulatur. –

[1a] (*reading*)

"A song hath 'bars', as the Masters teach,
Which duly present a measure each:
For this are sundry stanzas needed,
With laws that must be heeded.
In a stanza, first you put together
Two strophes, sung to one melody;
And each to several lines extend,
Each line or verse a rhyme must end.

"Ein jedes Meistergesanges Bar
stell' ordentlich ein Gemässe dar
aus unterschiedlichen Gesetzen,
die Keiner soll verletzen.
Ein Gesetz besteht aus zweenen Stollen,
die gleiche Melodei haben sollen;
der Stoll' aus etlicher Vers' Gebänd',
der Vers hat seinen Reim am End'.

There follows then the Aftersong,   Darauf so folgt der Abgesang,
Which is several verses long.   der sei auch etlich' Verse lang,
This also must have its melody,   und hab' sein' besondere Melodei,
But this must not like the strophe be.   als nicht im Stollen zu finden sei.
The songs with 'bars' of such a measure,   Derlei Gemässes mehre Baren
As Mastersongs we duly treasure.   soll ein jed' Meisterlied bewahren;
Of sequent notes as used before,   und wer ein neues Lied gericht',
Our rules allow not more than four.   das über vier der Sylben nicht
Who sings a song upon this wise   eingreift in andrer Meister Weis',
Shall gain thereby the Master's prize."   des' Lied erwerb' sich Meister-Preis." –

(*He gives the board back to the prentices: they hang it again on the wall.*)

Be seated in the singer's chair!   Nun setzt euch in den Singestuhl!

WALTHER
(*with a shudder*)

Here in this chair?   Hier in den Stuhl?

KOTHNER

'Tis custom here!   Wie's Brauch der Schul'.

WALTHER
(*He seats himself unwillingly.*)
(*aside*)

For thee, beloved, this shall be!   Für dich, Geliebte, sei's gethan!

KOTHNER
(*very loud*)

The singer sits.   Der Sänger sitzt.

BECKMESSER
(*invisible, from the Marker's dais, but very loud*)

Now begin!   Fanget an!

WALTHER
(*after a short consideration*)

"Now begin!"   [17]   Fanget an!
So cried the spring through the land: [6a]   So rief der Lenz in den Wald,
Loud echoed her command,   dass laut es ihn durchhallt;
And through the forest flying, [19]   und wie in ferneren Wellen
Scarce reached its farthest bound,   der Hall von dannen flieht,
When distant glens replying   von weither nahet ein Schwellen,
Gave back a mighty sound.   das mächtig näher zieht;
  The woods ere long [16c]   es schwillt und schallt,
  Are filled with song   es tönt der Wald
And sweetly sounding voices;   von holder Stimmen Gemenge;
  Now loud and clear   nun laut und hell
  The sound draws near;   schon nah' zur Stell',
  The tumult swells   wie wächst der Schwall!
  Like pealing bells,   Wie Glockenhall
And every creature rejoices!   ertos't des Jubels Gedränge!
  All heard   Der Wald,
  Spring's word   wie bald
And answered to her call,   antwortet er dem Ruf
New life she'd given all,   der neu ihm Leben schuf,
  Raised on high   stimmte an
The tender song of spring! –   das süsse Lenzes – Lied! –

(*During this, repeated groans of discouragement and scratchings of chalk are heard from the Marker. Walther hears them, and, after a momentary pause of discomposure, continues.*)

Deep in the thorny cover,   In einer Dornenhecken,
Consumed by wrath and hate,   von Neid und Gram verzehrt,
When now his reign is over,   muss' er sich da verstecken,
Old Winter lies in wait;   der Winter, Grimm-bewehrt:
In gloom of deepest woods   von dürrem Laub umrauscht,
He cowers there and broods   er lauert da und lauscht,
How all this joyful singing   wie er das frohe Singen
He could to woe be bringing!   zu Schaden könnte bringen –

(*He stands up in displeasure.*)

But, now begin!	Doch: fanget an!
So rang the cry in my breast,	So rief es mir in die Brust,
Before I had heard love's behest.	als noch ich von Liebe nicht wusst'.
I thought I woke from dreaming;	Da fühlt' ich's tief sich regen,
Deep down my spirit was thrilled,	als weckt' es mich aus dem Traum;
My fevered pulse was leaping,	mein Herz mit bebenden Schlägen
My being with joy was filled:	erfüllte des Busens Raum:
My blood on fire	das Blut, es wall't
With wild desire,	mit Allgewalt,
Some new emotion thronging;	geschwellt von neuem Gefühle;
Through sultry night,	aus warmer Nacht
With greatest might,	mit Uebermacht
Tempests of sighs	schwillt mir zum Meer
In tumult rise	der Seufzer Heer
And tell my passion of longing;	in wildem Wonne-Gewühle:
I heard	die Brust,
Spring's word	mit Lust,
And answered to her call,	antwortet sie dem Ruf,
New life she'd given to all;	der neu ein Leben schuf:
Loud I sang	stimmt nun an
The glorious song of love!	das hehre Liebes-Lied!

BECKMESSER
(who has grown more restive, tears open the curtains)

Well, have you finished?	18 Seid ihr nun fertig?

WALTHER

Why do you ask?	Wie fraget ihr?

BECKMESSER
(harshly)

See, the slate here with your faults is full.	Mit der Tafel ward ich fertig schier.

[16a] (*He hold out the slate quite covered with chalk marks; the Masters laugh.*)

WALTHER

But wait! Unto my lady's praise	Hört doch! Zu meiner Frauen Preis
A fitting lay now would I raise.	gelang' ich jetzt erst mit der Weis'.

BECKMESSER
(leaving his position)

Sing where you will! Here, fixed is your fate!	Singt, wo ihr wollt! Hier habt ihr verthan. –
Ye Masters, turn your eyes on the slate! [20a]Ihr Meister, schaut die Tafel euch an:	
The like of this was never heard!	so lang' ich leb', ward's nicht erhört;
No never, though you pledge your word!	ich glaubt's nicht, wenn ihr's All' auch schwört!

(*The Masters are in commotion.*)

WALTHER

I ask you, Master, is this not wrong?	Erlaubt ihr's Meister, dass er mich stört?
May no-one hear me end my song?	Blieb ich von Allen ungehört?

POGNER

One word, Sir Marker! Be not unjust.	Ein Wort, Herr Merker! Ihr seid gereizt!

BECKMESSER

Be Marker henceforth whoever will	Sei Merker fortan, wer darnach geizt
But, that the knight has failed beyond all doubt,	Doch dass der Ritter versungen hat,
That will I prove to all the Master's guild.	beleg' ich erst noch vor der Meister Rath.
But heavy toil the task will be!	Zwar wird's 'ne harte Arbeit sein:
Where begin it, what sense no man can see?	wo beginnen, da wo nicht aus noch ein?
Mistakes in quantity and rhyme	Von falscher Zahl, und falschem Gebänd'
This time I will ignore;	schweig' ich schon ganz und gar;
Too short, too long, with no thought for time.	zu kurz, zu lang, wer ein End' da fänd'!

Have you heard such nonsense before? / Wer meint hier im Ernst einen Bar?
His "hazy meaning" – that's bad enough! / Auf "blinde Meinung" klag' ich allein:
Tell me, what sense you find in this stuff? / sagt, konnt' ein Sinn unsinniger sein?

MASTERSINGERS

I found no sense! I must confess, / Man wird nicht klug! Ich muss gesteh'n,
None there could find an end, I confess. / Ein Ende konnte Keiner erseh'n.

BECKMESSER

And then the mode, what medley it showed / Und dann die Weis'! Welch tolles Gekreis'
Of "bold adventure-", "blue rider-spur-" / aus "Abenteuer-", "blau Rittersporn-"
   mode, /   Weis',
"High firtree-", "proud stripling-" tone! / "hoch Tannen-" und "stolz Jüngling-"
    /   Ton!

KOTHNER

I understood nothing at all. / Ja, ich verstand gar nichts davon!

BECKMESSER

No pause or form, no coloratur, / Kein Absatz wo, kein' Coloratur
Of melody no trace could I hear! / von Melodei auch nicht eine Spur!

MASTERSINGERS
(becoming more and more excited)

Who calls that a song?   [6a,b]   Wer nennt das Gesang?
We listen too long! / 's ward einem bang!
Empty noise I find it! / Eitel Ohrgeschinder!
There's nothing behind it! / Gar nichts dahinter!

KOTHNER

And from his seat he jumps while he's / Und gar vom Singstuhl ist er gesprungen!
   singing!

BECKMESSER

D'you wish me to show what I have / Wird erst auf die Fehlerprobe gedrungen?
   detected,
Or at once declare he is rejected? / Oder gleich erklärt, dass er versungen?

SACHS
(who from the start listened to Walther with increasing eagerness, comes forward.)

Stay, Master! Why so much haste? / Halt! Meister! Nicht so geeilt!
Not everyone can share your taste. / Nicht Jeder eure Meinung theilt. –
   The singer's bold intention,   [21a]   Des Ritters Lied und Weise,
I found it new, but hardly wrong. / sie fand ich neu, doch nicht verwirrt;
   Though he has scorned convention, /   verliess er uns're G'leise,
His step was firm and ever strong. / schritt er doch fest und unbeirrt.
   If by the rules you'd measure /   Wollt ihr nach Regeln messen,
What does not with your rules agree; / was nicht nach eurer Regeln Lauf,
   Forget the laws you treasure, /   der eig'nen Spur vergessen,
Seek out first what his rules may be. / sucht davon erst die Regeln auf!

BECKMESSER

Aha, 'tis well! Now hear him, pray!   [20]   Aha! Schon recht! Nun hört ihr's doch:
For Sachs to bunglers shows the way, / den Stümpern öffnet Sachs ein Loch,
   Where they may roam at their pleasure, /   da aus und ein nach Belieben
   With none to take their measure! /   ihr Wesen leicht sie trieben.
Sing to the mob in the streets and the / Singet dem Volk auf Markt und Gassen;
   market
Here singers are ruled by the laws of singing. / hier wird nach den Regeln nur eingelassen!

SACHS

Friend Marker, why so hotly burning? / Herr Merker, was doch solch ein Eifer?
   You are upset, I fear! /   Was doch so wenig Ruh'?
Your judgement might be more discerning / Eu'r Urtheil, dünkt mich, wäre reifer,
Had you a keener ear! / hörtet ihr besser zu!
And so, now hear my final word, / Darum, so komm' ich jetzt zum Schluss,
That the singer to the end must be heard. / dass den Junker zu End' man hören muss.

The Masters' Guild and all the schools,
Set against Sachs are nought but fools!

Der Meister Zunft, die ganze Schul',
gegen den Sachs da sind wie Null!

SACHS

Now God forbid that I should claim
To flout our laws or deny their aim!
'Tis written in this fashion:
"The Marker shall be chosen so,
    That, free from hate and passion,
He may not swerve for friend or foe."
Now if our Marker goes a-wooing;
Can he refrain his best from doing
To brand his rival on the stool
And shame him here before the school!

Verhüt es Gott, was ich begehr',
dass das nicht nach den Gesetzen wär'!
    Doch da nun steht's geschrieben,
der Merker werde so bestellt,
    dass weder Hass noch Lieben
das Urtheil trüben, das er fällt.
[15] Geht der nun gar auf Freiers-Füssen,
wie sollt' er da die Lust nicht büssen,
den Nebenbuhler auf dem Stuhl
zu schmähen vor der ganzen Schul'?

(*Walther flames up.*)

NACHTIGALL

You go too far!

Ihr geht zu weit!

KOTHNER

Of wrath beware!

Persönlichkeit!

POGNER
(*to the Mastersingers*)

I pray you, Masters, no more strife!

Vermeidet, Meister, Zwist und Streit!

BECKMESSER

Ei! What is it to Master Sachs, then,
    How I may see fit to go?
Let him rather give heed to his cobbling,
    And make a better shoe!
But since my cobbler has taken to verse,
The shoes he makes have grown worse and
    worse;
        Unsound throughout,
        They flap all about!
    This stuff he loves to scrawl,
    He can just keep it all,
His lays and plays, his farcical muse,
If he'll just bring me my fine new shoes! [??a]

Ei, was kümmert's doch Meister Sachsen,
    auf was für Füssen ich geh'?
Liess' er d'rob lieber Sorge sich wachsen,
    dass nichts mir drück' die Zeh'!
Doch seit mein Schuster ein grosser Poet,
gar übel es um mein Schuhwerk steht;
        da seht, wie es schlappt,
        und überall klappt!
    All' seine Vers' und Reim'
    liess' ich ihm gern daheim,
Historien, Spiel' und Schwänke dazu,
brächt' er mir morgen die neuen Schuh'!

SACHS
(*scratching*)

That's true I must admit,
    But do you think it fit
That if I write a paltry verse
    On the donkey driver's shoe,
Our wise and learned Sir Town Clerk
    Should not have his verses too?
But verses worthy of your choice,
Among all the humble poems I voice,
    Found I as yet not one!
    But now perhaps 'twill come,
After Sir Walther's song I've heard,
So let him sing on now undisturbed!

Ihr mahnt mich da gar recht:
    doch schickt sich's, Meister, sprecht,
dass, find' ich selbst dem Eseltreiber
    ein Sprüchlein auf die Sohl',
dem hochgelahrten Herrn Stadtschreiber
    ich nichts d'rauf schreiben soll?
Das Sprüchlein, das eu'r würdig sei,
mit all' meiner armen Poeterei
    fand ich noch nicht zur Stund';
    doch wird's wohl jetzt mir kund,
wenn ich des Ritters Lied gehört: –
d'rum sing' er nun weiter ungestört!

(*Walther jumps on the Singer's chair in great excitement and looks down.*)

BECKMESSER

No further! An end!

Nichts weiter! Zum Schluss!

MASTERSINGERS

No more! An end!

Genug! Zum Schluss!

SACHS
(*to Walther*)

Sing just to make the Marker roar!

Singt, dem Herrn Merker zum Verdruss!

67

BECKMESSER

(As Walther begins again, Beckmesser shows his slate to the Masters, who gather round him in a circle.)

What use then is all our schooling?	Was sollte man da noch hören?
Such singing is but fooling!	Wär's nicht nur uns zu bethören?
Every fault both great and small!	Jeden der Fehler gross und klein,
Look you here, do but see the slate.	seht genau auf der Tafel ein. –
"Faulty verse," "unsingable phrases,"	"Falsch Gebänd," "unredbare Worte,"
"Word clippings," I reprehend!	"Kleb-Sylben," hier "Laster" gar;
"Aequivocal!" "rhymes in unfit places."	"Aequivoca," "Reim am falschen Orte,"
"Reversed", "misplaced," from end to end!	"verkehrt," "verstellt" der ganze Bar;
A "patchwork-song" here, filling the pauses!	ein "Flickgesang" hier zwischen den Stollen;
"Hazy meaning," see, everywhere!	"blinde Meinung" allüberall;
"Unmeaning words," "breaking off" "lame clauses",	"unklare Wort", "Differenz," hie "Schrollen,"
There "faulty breathing," "surprises" here!	da "falscher Athem," hier "Ueberfall."
A mixing up of all tones that be.	Aus allen Tönen ein Mischgebräu'!
Incomprehensible melody!	Ganz unverständliche Melodei!
If you are equal to the strain	Scheu'tet ihr nicht das Ungemach,
Masters, count all his faults again!	Meister, zählt mir die Striche nach!
Already at the eight he was cast,	Verloren hätt' er schon mit dem acht':
But so long as he, sure no man did e'er last:	doch so weit wie der hat's noch Keiner gebracht!
Well over fifty, that is clear!	Wohl über fünfzig, schlecht gezählt!
Say, shall now the knight be Master here?	Sagt, ob ihr euch den zum Meister wählt?

MASTERSINGERS
(to one another)

Ah yes, how true; for with each verse	Ja wohl, so ist's! Ich seh' es recht!
The young knight goes from bad to worse!	Mit dem Herrn Ritter steht es schlecht.
Let Sachs think of him as he may choose,	Mag Sachs von ihm halten, was er will,
To make him Master we refuse!	hier in der Singschul' schweig' er still!
Shall any Master, spite our denial,	Bleibt einem jeden doch unbenommen,
As Master choose whomever he will?	wen er zum Genossen begehrt?
May all come in without a trial?	Wär uns der erste Best' willkommen,
What good is then to Masters their skill?	was blieben die Meister dann werth? –
Hei! See how the knight is distraught!	Hei! Wie sich der Ritter da quält!
Though Sachs for him well has fought!	Der Sachs hat ihn sich erwählt! –
'Tis not to be borne! Now make an end!	's ist ärgerlich gar! D'rum macht ein End'!
Each Master, speak, and uplift his hand!	Auf, Meister, stimmt und erhebt die Händ'!

POGNER
(aside)

Ah yes, indeed, right well I see,	Ja wohl, ich seh's, was mir nicht recht:
My knight will ne'er a Master be!	mit meinem Junker steht es schlecht!
If I should be overborne,	Weiche ich hier der Uebermacht,
I fear the outcome I shall mourn.	mir ahnet, dass mir's Sorge macht.
How gladly would I welcome him.	Wie gerne säh' ich ihn angenommen,
Such kinsman would I not refuse:	als Eidam wär' er mir gar werth;
But when the winner comes a-wooing,	nenn' ich den Sieger nun willkommen,
Who knows if him my child will choose?	wer weiss, ob ihn mein Kind begehrt!
I fear me when he woos,	Gesteh' ich's, dass mich das quält,
That maid his suit will refuse!	ob Eva den Meister wählt!

WALTHER
(in wild and desperate enthusiasm, standing on the Singer's chair and looking down on the commotion of the Mastersingers.)

Now from the thorny thicket	Aus finst'rer Dornenhecken
The owl flies through the wood,	Die Eule rauscht' hervor,
With hoots and cries he wakens	thät rings mit Kreischen wecken
The raven's croaking brood:	der Raben heis'ren Chor:
Now calls the dusky crowd	in nächt'gem Heer zu Hauf
To rise and shriek aloud:	wie krächzen all' da auf,

With voices hoarse and hollow,	mit ihren Stimmen, den hohlen,
The crows and jackdaws follow!	die Elstern, Kräh'n und Dohlen!
Up then soars	Auf da steigt
On golden pinions borne,	mit gold'nem Flügelpaar
A bird to greet the morn,	ein Vogel wunderbar:
With wondrous plumage o'er me [19]	sein strahlend hell Gefieder
Serene in Heaven high;	licht in den Lüften blinkt;
It gleams and floats before me,	schwebt selig hin und wieder,
And lures me on to fly. [6a]	zu Flug und Flucht mir winkt.
Now swells my heart	Es schwillt das Herz
With tender smart,	von süssem Schmerz,
As wings by need are given:	der Noth entwachsen Flügel;
To mountain height	es schwinkt sich auf
In dauntless flight,	zum kühnen Lauf,
From the city's tomb,	zum Flug durch die Luft
Towards its home,	aus der Städte Gruft,
Its wings are surely driven,	dahin zum heim'schen Hügel;
To meadows where the song of birds,	dahin zur grünen Vogelweid',
The Master first revealed in words;	wo Meister Walther einst mich freit';
Where I my song will raise	da sing' ich hell und hehr
In fairest woman's praise:	der liebsten Frauen Ehr':
There on high,	auf da steigt,
Though raven Masters croak and cry,	ob Meister-Kräh'n ihm ungeneigt,
My song of love shall swell!	das stolze Minne-Lied. –
On earth, ye Masters, farewell!	Ade! ihr Meister, hienied'!

(Walther, with a proudly contemptuous gesture, jumps off the chair and quickly turns to go.)

SACHS
(observing Walther with rapture)

Ah! What a fire	Ha, welch ein Muth!
The heavens inspire! –	Begeist'rungs-Gluth! –
Ye Masters, let him be heard!	Ihr Meister, schweigt doch und hört!
Hear, if Sachs gives his word! –	Hört, wenn Sachs euch beschwört! –
Sir Marker there, let us have rest!	Herr Merker da! gönnt doch nur Ruh'!
Let others hear him; grant that at least! –	Lasst And're hören! gebt das nur zu! –
In vain! A vain endeavour!	Umsonst! All eitel Trachten!
Nought is heard, I may hold my tongue;	Kaum vernimmt man sein eigen Wort!
No use though he sing forever:	Des Junkers will Keiner achten: –
In truth, 'tis brave, striving so long!	dass heiss' ich Muth, singt der noch fort!
With heart in its place aright,	Das Herz auf dem rechten Fleck:
A true-born poet knight! –	ein wahrer Dichter-Reck'!
Hans Sachs may make both verse and shoe,	Mach' ich, Hans Sachs, wohl Vers' und Schuh',
But knight is he, knight and poet too.	ist Ritter der und Poet dazu.

PRENTICES
(who have been rubbing their hands in glee, jump up from the bench, take hands towards the end and dance around the Marker's dais.)

Good luck to Mastersinging,	Glück auf zum Meistersingen,
Your garland then may you be winning;	mögt' ihr euch das dränzlein erschwingen!
The silken garland of flowers bright,	Das Blumenkränzlein aus Seiden fein,
Will that by good fortune be yours, Sir Knight?	wird das dem Herrn Ritter beschieden sein?

BECKMESSER

Now Masters, judge aright!	Nun, Meister, Kündet's an!

(Most of them hold up their hands.)

MASTERSINGERS

Rejected is the knight!	Versungen und verthan!

General excitement: the prentices arm themselves with pieces of the Marker's dais, the chair and the benches, and cause confusion among the Masters who are making for the door. Sachs, who has remained alone in front, still gazes thoughtfully at the empty singer's chair. The boys remove this and, as Sachs turns away with a humourously indignant gesture, the curtain falls.
[1a]

Act Two

Scene One. *The stage represents the intersection of a narrow crooked alley, winding from the back, with a street which runs from side to side; one of the two corner houses belongs to Pogner, the other to Sachs. A short flight of steps leads up to Pogner's front door, which has a porch with stone seats in it. To the right, a lime tree shades the house, and bushes surround another stone seat at its foot. Sachs's house may be entered from the street – a divided door leads straight into the workshop, which is overshadowed by an elder tree. Two windows, one to the workshop, the other to an inner room, give onto the alley. (All houses both in the street and alley must be practicable.)*
A balmy summer evening: during the first scene, night gradually falls. David and other prentices are putting up the shutters.

PRENTICES
(during their work)

Midsummer day! Midsummer day!	Johannistag! Johannistag!
Flowers and ribbons wear while you may!	Blumen and Bänder so viel man mag!

DAVID
(aside, softly)

"The silken garland of flowers fine	"Das Blumenkränzlein von Seiden fein,
Would that tomorrow it might be mine!"	möcht' es mir balde beschieden sein!"

MAGDALENE
(Coming from Pogner's house with a basket on her arm, she tries to approach David without him seeing her.)

Hist! David!	Bst! David!

DAVID
(turning towards the alley)

Still are you calling?	Ruft ihr schon wieder?
Why should I sing your silly ditties!	Singt allein eure dummen Lieder!

(He turns angrily away.)

PRENTICES

David give ear.	David was soll's?
Proud be not here:	Wär'st nicht so stolz,
Turn but your eyes,	schaut'st besser um,
If you are wise!	wär'st nicht so dumm!
"Midsummer day! Midsummer day!"	"Johannistag! Johannistag!"
And he cannot see his Lene, and turns away!	Wie nur die Jungfer Lene nicht kennen mag!

MAGDALENE

David! Listen! Turn round my dear!	David! hör' doch! kehr' dich zu mir!

DAVID

Ah, Magdalene, you are here.	Ach, Junfer Lene! Ihr seid hier?

MAGDALENE
(pointing to her basket)

Look in and see what is inside;	Bring' dir was Gut's; schau' nur hinein!
I brought it for my sweetheart dear.	Das soll für mein lieb' Schätzel sein. –
But tell me first, what luck had Sir Walther?	Erst aber schnell, wie ging's mit dem Ritter?
You gave him advice? Did he win the crown?	Du riethest ihm gut? Er gewann den Kranz?

DAVID

Ah, Magdalene! 'Twas unlucky,	Ach, Junger Lene! Da steht's bitter;
He was rejected and shouted down.	der hat verthan und versungen ganz!

70

(alarmed)

Rejected? No hope?   Versungen? Verthan?

DAVID

What is that to you?   Was geht's euch nur an?

MAGDALENE
(quickly pulling back her basket as David reaches for it)

Hands from the basket!   Hand von der Taschen!
Do not touch it!   Nichts da zu naschen! –
Alas! Now misfortune I see!   Hilf Gott! Unser Junker verthan!

(She hurries back into the house, wringing her hands in despair. David looks after her dumbfounded.)

PRENTICES
(who have crept near to listen, pretend to congratulate David.)

Hail! Hail! Our young man wants to wed!   Heil, Heil zur Eh' dem jungen Mann!
How kindly he is received!   Wie glücklich hat er gefrei't!
We heard and saw all that was said.   Wir hörten's All', und sahen's an:
He offered her his heart,   der er sein Herz geweiht,
His life if she'd but ask it,   für die er lässt sein Leben,
But she would not give him her basket!   die hat ihm den Korb nicht gegeben.

DAVID
(angrily)

Go back to your work!   Was steht ihr hier faul?
Stop fooling about!   Gleich haltet eu'r Maul!

PRENTICES
(They make a ring and dance around him.)

"Midsummer day! Midsummer day!"   Johannistag! Johannistag!
Each man must wed as best he may: Da frei't ein Jeder wie er mag.
The master weds,   Der Meister freit!
The prentice weds,   der Bursche freit,
Fortune will follow the bold ones!   Da gibt's Geschlamb' und Geschlumbfer!
When grey-beards wed   Der Alte freit
The youngest maids   die junge Maid,
The prentices wed the old ones!   der Bursche die alte Jumbfer! –
Juchhei! Juchhei! Midsummer day!   Juchhei! Juchhei! Johannistag!

(David is on the point of fighting the boys when Sachs, who has come up the alley, intervenes. The Prentices disperse.)

SACHS
(to David)

What's this? Must you be always in fights? [22a] Was gibt's? Treff' ich dich wieder am
                                                 Schlag?

DAVID

Not I, they were all teasing me!   Nicht ich! Schandlieder singen die.

SACHS

Pay no heed, learn better than they!   Hör nicht d'rauf! Lern's besser wie sie! –
Go in, lock up! Bring me a light!   Zur Ruh'! in's Haus! Schliess' und mach'
                                            Licht!

DAVID

Have I to sing now?   Hab' ich noch Singstund'?

SACHS

No, no song   Nein, singst nicht!
To pay for your cheeky interruptions!   [11] Zur Straf für dein heutig' frech' Erdreisten.
Now on the last, put the shoes and leave me! Die neuen Schuh' steck' auf den Leisten!

(They go through the workshop into the house.)

Scene Two. *Pogner and Eva, returning from a walk, come in silence up the alley, Eva leaning lightly on her father's arm.*

3

POGNER
(peeping through a chink in Sachs's shutter)

We'll see if Master Sachs is there.	Lass seh'n, ob Meister Sachs zu Haus? –
I'd speak with him: shall I go in?	Gern spräch' ich ihn. Trät' ich wohl ein?

(David comes from the inner room with a light and sits at the work-bench by the window to work.)

EVA
(peeping)

I think he's in: his light still shines.	Er scheint daheim: kommt Licht heraus.

POGNER

Shall I? – What use though? – Better not!	Thu' ich's? – Zu was doch? – Besser, nein!

(He turns away.)

On entering some new venture,	Will Einer Selt'nes wagen,
No man wants words of censure,	was liess' er da sich sagen? –

(after some reflection)

And he 'twas who said I went too far?	War er's nicht, der meint', ich ging zu weit?
And yet old custom not heeding,	Und blieb ich nicht im Geleise,
I followed on his leading?	war's nicht in seiner Weise? –
But yet perhaps 'twas vanity?	Doch war's vielleicht auch – Eitelkeit? –

(He turns to Eva.)

And thou, my child? Hast thou no word?	Und du, mein Kind, du sagst mir nichts?

EVA

A child obeys and is not heard.	Ein folgsam Kind, gefragt nur spricht's.

POGNER
(very tenderly)

How wise! How good! Come, sit down here	Wie klug! Wie gut! – Komm', setz' dich hier
And talk a while with me my child.	ein' Weil' noch auf die Bank zu mir.

(He sits on the bench under the lime tree.)

EVA

Is it not too cool?	Wird's nicht zu kühl?
Though the day's been warm.	's war heut' gar schwül.

(She sits beside Pogner, hesitating and anxious.)

POGNER

Ah no, the air is kindly,	Nicht doch, 's ist mild und labend;
And soft the night and friendly:	gar lieblich lind der Abend.
'Tis promise that the fairest day	Das deutet auf den schönsten Tag,
Tomorrow will be dawning.	der morgen dir soll scheinen.
O child! Does not thy heart tell thee,	O Kind, sagt dir kein Herzensschlag,
What joy tomorrow thine may be,	welch' Glück dich morgen treffen mag,
When Nuremberg in all her state,	[23] wenn Nürnberg, die ganze Stadt
With acclamations ringing,	mit Bürgern und Gemeinen,
Will come, with folk both small and great,	mit Zünften, Volk und hohem Rath,
To see thee crown our singing,	vor dir sich soll vereinen,
And thou as bride	dass du den Preis,
Shalt crown the man	das edle Reis,
Who gaineth thee as prize,	ertheilest als Gemahl
The Master of thy choice?	dem Meister deiner Wahl?

EVA

Dear father, must he a Master be?	Lieb' Vater, muss es ein Meister sein?

POGNER

Yes child, but only of thy choice.	Hör' wohl: ein Meister deiner Wahl.

(Magdalene appears at the door and beckons to Eva.)

EVA
(absent-minded ly)

Yes, of my choice. – But now go in –	Ja, – meiner Wahl. – Doch, tritt nun ein –

(aloud turning to Magdalene)

Yes, Lene, yes, 'tis supper time!	Gleich, Lene, gleich! – zum Abendmahl.

(She rises.)

POGNER
(rising irritably)

But we have no guest?	's giebt doch keinen Gast?

EVA
(as before)

Not Sir Walther?	Wohl den Junker?

POGNER
(surprised)

How so?	Wie so?

EVA

Did you not see him?	Sahst ihn heut' nicht?

POGNER
(half aside)

He pleased me not.	Ward sein' nicht froh. –

(meditatively and absently, then collecting himself and tapping his forehead)

But yet! – What now? – Ah! I'm a fool!	Nicht doch! – Was denn? – Ei! werd' ich dumm!

EVA

Dear father, now quick! Go change your gown.	Lieb' Väterchen, komm'! Geh', kleid' dich um.

POGNER
(as he goes before her into the house)

Hm! What thoughts in my head go round?	Hm! – Was geht mir im Kopf doch 'rum?

(Exit.)

MAGDALENE
(furtively to Eva)

What have you heard?	Hast was heraus?

EVA
(also furtively)

No word he spoke.	Blieb still und stumm.

MAGDALENE

My David says your lover has failed.	Sprach David: Meint', er habe verthan.

EVA
(alarmed)

Sir Walther? Ah me! What shall I do?	Der Ritter! – Hilf Gott, was fing' ich an?
Ah, Lene, my fears! How to allay them?	Ach, Lene die Angst! Wo 'was erfahren?

MAGDALENE

Perhaps from Sachs?	Vielleicht vom Sachs?

EVA
(cheerfully)

Ah! He loves me well:	Ach, der hat mich lieb!
To him I will go.	Gewiss, ich geh' hin.

MAGDALENE

Beware of your father,	Lass' drin nichts gewahren!
For he will notice if you are late.	Der Vater merkt' es, wenn man jetzt blieb'. –
In a while, I'll meet you and tell you a secret	Nach dem Mahl: dann hab' ich dir noch 'was zu sagen
That someone confided to me lately.	was Jemand geheim mir aufgetragen.

EVA
(turning round)

Who then? Sir Walther? Wer denn? Der Junker?

MAGDALENE

Not he! No! Nichts da! Nein!
Beckmesser. Beckmesser.

EVA

A pretty secret, that! Das mag 'was Rechtes sein!

(She goes into the house. Magdalene follows her.)

Scene Three. *Sachs, in his shirtsleeves, has returned from the inner room to the shop. He turns to David who is still at his bench.*

SACHS

Let's see, that's good. – Here in the light
Put my stool and table now outside.
Then go to bed, be up in time:
Sleep off your folly, tomorrow be wise!

Zeig' her! – 's ist gut. – Dort an die Thür'
rück' mir Tisch und Schemel herfür! –
Leg' dich zu Bett! Wach' auf bei Zeit,
verschlaf' die Dummheit, sei morgen
gescheit!

DAVID
(as he arranges the bench and stool)

More work this evening? Schafft ihr noch Arbeit?

SACHS

What's it to you? Kümmert dich das?

DAVID
(aside)

What's wrong now with Lene? – Goodness
knows.
But why does the Master work tonight?

Was war nur der Lene? – Gott weiss, was! –
[22a]Warum wohl der Meister heute wacht?

SACHS

You still here? Was steh'st noch?

DAVID

Sleep well, Master! Schlaft wohl, Meister!

SACHS

Good night! Gut' Nacht!

(David goes into the inner room. Sachs sits on the stool by the door and arranges his work; then, laying it aside, he leans back, his arm resting on the closed lower half of the door.) [19]

The elder's scent how tender,
How mild, how rich it falls!
It bids my soul surrender,
Words from out my heart it calls.
And yet such words are hard to find
For one like me, simple of mind!
Though for my work I've no liking,
Good friend, let me go free;
I'd better get back to my working,
And let all this poetry be!

Wie duftet doch der Flieder
so mild, so stark und voll!
Mir lös't es weich die Glieder,
will dass ich was sagen soll. –
Was gilt's, was ich dir sagen kann?
Bin gar ein arm einfältig Mann!
Soll mir die Arbeit nicht schmecken,
gäb'st, Freund, lieber mich frei:
thät' besser das Leder zu strecken,
und liess alle Poeterei, –

[29]

(He begins to work abruptly and noisily, then breaks off again and leans back thoughtfully.)

And yet it haunts me still.
I feel, yet follow it ill,
Cannot forget it and still cannot grasp it,
It slips from my hand, even when I clasp
it.
But yet how could I measure
What no earthly measure could fit?

Und doch, 's will halt nicht geh'n. –
Ich fühl's – und kann's nicht versteh'n –
kann's nicht behalten, – doch auch nicht
vergessen;
und fass' ich es ganz – kann ich's nicht
messen! –
[4] Doch wie auch wollt' ich's fassen,
was unermesslich mir schien?

It flouted rules that we treasure,	Kein' Regel wollte da passen,
Yet in it no fault I find.	und war doch kein Fehler drin. –
It seemed so old, yet new did it ring,	[6a,b]Es klang so alt, und war doch so neu, –
Like morning song of birds in spring.	[5] wie Vogelsang in süssen Mai: –
One who heard,	wer ihn hört,
And madly dared	und wahnbethört
That song to sing again,	sänge dem Vogel nach,
Would reap but scorn and shame.	dem brächt' es Spott und Schmach. –
Spring's sweetest strain, [17]	Lenzes Gebot,
Its wondrous pain,	die süsse Noth,
These taught him what he must say:	die legten's ihm in die Brust:
Then sang he in Nature's way,	nun sang er, wie er musst'!
And Nature's way he captured –	Und wie er musst', so konnt' er's;
I saw him so enraptured.	das merkt' ich ganz besonders:
The bird who sang today,	dem Vogel, der heut' sang,
From Mother Nature learned his singing;	dem war der Schnabel hold gewachsen;
Masters may show dismay,	macht' er den Meistern bang,
Hans Sachs will ever hear it ringing!	gar wohl gefiel er doch Hans Sachsen.

(He resumes his work cheerfully.)

✓ **Scene Four.** *Eva comes into the street and shyly approaches Sachs's shop, where she stands unnoticed.*

EVA

| Good evening, Master! You're still working? | Gut'n Abend, Meister! Noch so fleissig? |

SACHS
(starts with pleasure)

Ah child! Sweet Eva, still awake?	Ei, Kind! Lieb' Evchen? Noch so spät?
And yet I think I know the reason, [24]	Und doch, warum so spät noch, weiss ich:
The new-made shoes?	die neuen Schuh'?

EVA

You are quite wrong!	Wie fehl er räth!
The shoes hardly have been in my mind;	Die Schuh' hab' ich noch gar nicht probiert;
They are so fine, so richly made	die sind so schön, so reich geziert,
That they on my feet have not even been tried.	dass ich sie noch nicht an die Füss' mir getraut.

(She seats herself near Sachs on the stone seat.) [26]

SACHS

| Tomorrow you will wear them as bride? | Doch sollst sie morgen tragen als Braut? |

EVA

| But who will the bridegroom be? | Wer wäre denn Bräutigam? |

SACHS

| Who can tell? | Weiss ich das? |

EVA

| Can you say I'll be a bride? | Wie wisst denn ihr, dass ich Braut? |

SACHS

| Ah well, | Ei was! |
| Everyone knows. | Das weiss die Stadt. |

EVA

Yes, everyone knows,	Ja, weiss es die Stadt,
Friend Sachs wiser and wiser grows!	Freund Sachs gute Gewähr dann hat.
I thought he knew more.	Ich dacht', er wüsst' mehr.

SACHS

| What should I know then? | Was sollt' ich wissen? |

EVA	
Ah, look now! Must I my secret show you?	Ei seht doch! Werd' ich's ihm sagen müssen?
Am I, then, so dull?	Ich bin wohl recht dumm?

SACHS

I don't say that.	Das sag' ich nicht.

EVA

Are you then, so crafty?	Dann wär't ihr wohl klug?

SACHS

I don't know that.	Das weiss ich nicht.

EVA

You know naught! You say naught! Ah, friend Sachs,	Ihr wisst nichts? Ihr sagt nichts? – Ei, Freund Sachs,
Now I see truly, pitch is not wax.	jetzt merk' ich wahrlich, Pech ist kein Wachs.
I thought that your cunning was finer.	Ich hätt' euch für feiner gehalten.

SACHS

Child,	Kind!
Both wax and pitch are known to me;	Beid', Wachs und Pech vertraut mir sind.
The wax strengthens the silken stitching,	Mit Wachs strich ich die Seidenfäden,
With which for you those dainty shoes I sewed;	damit ich die zieren Schuh' dir gefasst:
Now I have some shoes that call for pitching,	heut' fass' ich die Schuh mit dicht'ren Drähten,
To help a clown on his stony road.	da gilt's mit Pech für den derben Gast.

EVA

Who, then, is he? Someone great?	Wer ist denn der? Wohl 'was rechts?

SACHS

Yes, truly.	Das mein' ich!
A Master proud who boldly woos,	Ein Meister stolz auf Freiers Fuss,
Expecting to triumph by his singing:	denkt morgen zu siegen ganz alleinig:
For Beckmesser's feet I make these shoes.	Herrn Beckmesser's Schuh' ich richten muss.

EVA

Then pitch in plenty let there be:	So nehmt nur tüchtig Pech dazu:
May he stick there and leave me free.	da kleb' er drin, und lass' mir Ruh'!

SACHS

He hopes to win you by his singing.	Er hofft dich sicher zu ersingen.

EVA

A man like that!	Wie so denn der?

SACHS

He's a bachelor.	Ein Junggesell'!
We have but few unmarried men.	's giebt deren wenig dort zur Stell'.

EVA

Might not a widower go a-wooing?	Könnt's einem Wittwer nicht gelingen?

SACHS

My child, he'd be too old for thee.	Mein Kind, der wär' zu alt für dich.

EVA

Ah, what! Too old? What wins is art;	Ei was, zu alt! Hier gilt's der Kunst:
And all who sing, to woo are free.	wer sie versteht, der werb' um mich!

SACHS

Don't try to pull wool over my eyes.	Lieb' Evchen! Machst mir blauen Dunst?

Not I, you; 'tis you that are cunning!

Your falseness you dare not deny.
Only God knows now who's taking your fancy.
For many a year I dreamed 'twas I.

Nicht ich! Ihr seid's; ihr macht mir Flausen!
Gesteht nur, dass ihr wandelbar;
Gott weiss, wer jetzt euch im Herzen mag hausen
Glaubt' ich mich doch drin so manches Jahr.

SACHS

Because in my arms oft I cradled you?

Wohl, da ich dich gern in den Armen trug?

EVA

I see. You had no child of your own.

Ich seh', 's war nur, weil ihr kinderlos.

SACHS
(softly)

I once had wife and children too!

Hatt' einst ein Weib und Kinder genug.

EVA

But dead is your wife and I am grown?

Doch starb eure Frau, so wuchs ich gross.

SACHS

So tall and fair!

Gar gross und schön!

EVA

　　　　The thought would come,
That I might be wife and child in one.

　　　　Drum dacht' ich aus:
ihr nähm't mich für Weib und Kind in's Haus.

SACHS

Then I should have child and also wife!
How happy then would be my life!
Yes, yes, your plot is quite clear to me!

Da hätt' ich ein Kind und auch ein Weib:
's wär gar ein lieber Zeitvertreib!
Ja ja! das hast du dir schön erdacht.

EVA

I think the Master is laughing at me?
I'm sure 'twill cause him but little sorrow,
If under his nose from all tomorrow,
Old Beckmesser wins me with his song.

Ich glaub', der Meister mich gar verlacht?
Am End' gar iess' er sich auch gefallen,
das unter der Nas' ihm weg von Allen
der Beckmesser morgen mich ersäng'?

SACHS

If he's successful, what can be done?
Only your father can advise.

Wie sollt' ich's wehren, wenn's ihm geläng'?
Dem wüsst' allein dein Vater Rath.

EVA

Where does a Master then keep his eyes?
Would I ask you now, if that were so?

Wo so ein Meister den Kopf nur hat!
Käm' ich zu euch wohl, fänd' ich's zu Haus?

SACHS
(drily)

Ah yes, how true, I am dense I know.
All day in thought I've tossed and turned,
But still it seems I've nothing learned.

Ach, ja! Hast Recht! 's ist im Kopf mir kraus:
hab' heut' manch' Sorg' un Wirr' erlebt:
da mag's dann sein, dass 'was drin klebt.

EVA
(again coming nearer)

Was't in the Song School? Today you met?

Wohl in der Singschul'? 's war heut' Gebot.

SACHS

Yes child, at that hearing I was upset.

Ja, Kind: eine Freiung machte mir Noth.

EVA

Ah Sachs! If only you'd mentioned the matter
I'd not have wearied you with my chatter.

But say, what man your favour has sought?

Ja, Sachs! Das hättet ihr gleich soll'n sagen;
plagt' euch dann nicht mit unnützen Fragen. –
Nun sagt, wer wär's, der Freiung begehrt?

SACHS

A nobleman, and quite untaught.	Ein Junker, Kind, gar unbelehrt.

EVA
(pretending to be ignorant)

A noble? Oh tell! And did he succeed?	[16a]Ein Junker? Mein, sagt! – und ward er gefreit?

SACHS

Oh no, my child, we disagreed.	Nichts da, mein Kind! 's gab gar viel Streit.

EVA

Oh Sachs, do tell, how did it go?	So sagt! Erzählt, wie ging es zu?
Can I be calm if it plagues you so?	Macht's euch Sorg', wie liess' mir es Ruh'? –
Did he have no luck then? Was he so wrong?	So bestand er übel und hat verthan?

SACHS

For the knight all hope of success is gone.	Ohne Gnad' versang der Herr Rittersmann.

MAGDALENE
(comes out of the house and calls softly)

Eva! Eva!	Bst! Evchen! Bst!

EVA
(eagerly turning to Sachs)

Is it hopeless? Why?	Ohne Gnade? Wie?
Is there no way that one could try?	Kein Mittel gäb's, das ihm gedieh?
Was he so wrong, so much at fault	Sang er so schlecht, so fehlervoll,
That none of the Masters would take his part?	dass nichts mehr zum Meister ihm helfen soll?

SACHS

My child, the one who meets such disaster,	Mein Kind, für den ist Alles verloren,
No Master will be in any land.	und Meister wird der in keinem Land;
For one who's born as a Master,	denn wer als Meister ward geboren,
Receives from his Masters no helping hand.	der hat unter Meistern den schlimmsten Stand.

MAGDALENE
(louder)

Your father calls.	Der Vater verlangt.

EVA
(with increasing earnestness)

Can he not be told	So sagt mir noch an,
If none of the Masters the knight would uphold?	ob keinen der Meister zum Freund er gewann?

SACHS

Would that be likely? Who'd be his friend,	Das wär' nicht übel! Freund ihm noch sein!
One who made all Masters feel they were small?	Ihm, vor dem All' sich fühlten so klein!
That haughty noble, devil take him!	Den Junker Hochmuth, lasst ihn laufen,
Let the world outside awake him!	mag er durch die Welt sich raufen:
What we have learnt with toil and care,	was wir erlernt mit Noth und Müh',
Let him leave us in peace to enjoy it.	dabei lasst uns in Ruh' verschnaufen!
Why must he come here and destroy it?	Hier renn' er nichts uns über'n Haufen.
His fortune, let him seek elsewhere!	Sein Glück ihm anderswo erblüh'!

EVA
(rising angrily)

Yes! Elsewhere then, 'twill come I know!	Ja, anderswo soll's ihm erblüh'n,
Though you may try to spoil his chances,	als bei euch garst'gen, neid'schen Mannsen;
Where hearts with loving ardour glow	wo warm die Herzen noch erglüh'n,
In spite of nasty Master Hanses!	trotz allen tück'schen Meister Hansen! –

(to Magdalene)

Yes, Lene, yes! I'm coming now,	Ja, Lene! Gleich! ich komme schon!

Fine consolation I get here!	Was trüg' ich hier für Trost davon?
The smell of pitch could do him harm,	Da riecht's nach Pech, dass Gott erbarm'!
Let him burn it and keep himself warm!	Brennt' er's lieber, da würd' er doch warm!

[22a]

(*In great excitement she crosses the street with Magdalene, pausing, much agitated, at the door.*)

SACHS
(*looks after her, nodding his head meaningfully*)

I thought as much, now I must help!	Das dacht' ich wohl. Nun heisst's: schaff' Rath!

(*He closes the upper half of the door so that only a little light shows, and so he can hardly be seen.*)

MAGDALENE

My dear, why are you not at home?	Hilf gott! was bleibst du nur so spät?
Your father called.	Der Vater rief.

EVA

You go instead	Geh' zu ihm ein:
And say that I am gone to bed.	ich sei zu Bett im Kämmerlein.

MAGDALENE

No, no, listen! This you should know!	Nicht doch! Hör' nur! Komm' ich dazu?
Beckmesser found me and would not go	Beckmesser fand mich: er lässt nicht Ruh',
Until I promised that I would bring you	zur Nacht sollst du dich an's Fenster neigen.
Tonight to your window, then he will sing you	er will dir was Schönes singen und geigen,
The song that he's hoping will win him the prize,	mit dem er dich hofft zu gewinnen, das Lied,
And earn him favour now in your eyes.	ob dir das zu Gefallen gerieth.

EVA

Must I bear that too! – I long for him.	Das fehlte auch noch! – Käme nur Er!

MAGDALENE

Has David been here?	Hast' David geseh'n?

EVA

What's he to me?	Was soll mir der?

(*She looks out.*)

MAGDALENE
(*aside*)

I was too hard; now he'll be pining.	Ich war zu streng; er wird sich grämen.

EVA

No one in sight?	Siehst du noch nichts?

MAGDALENE
(*appears to look out*)

It sounds like people coming.	's ist als ob Leut' dort kämen.

EVA

Walther!	Wär' er's?

MAGDALENE

Come, it's time to go in!	Mach' und komm' jetzt hinan!

EVA

Not yet, until I my dear one have seen!	Nicht eh'r, bis ich sah den theuersten Mann!

MAGDALENE

I made a mistake, it was not he.	Ich täuschte mich dort: er war es nicht. –
Now come, or soon your father will suspect!	Jetzt komm', sonst merkt der Vater die G'schicht'!

I'm so afraid!   Ach! meine Angst!

MAGDALENE

Now let us be thinking   Auch lass uns berathen,
How we can send that Beckmesser packing.   wie wir des Beckmesser's uns entladen.

EVA

Go to the window instead of me.   Zum Fenster gehst du für mich.

MAGDALENE

What? Me?   Wie, ich? –
(aside)
How great would be David's jealousy?   Das machte wohl David eiferlich?
He sleeps by the street there! Hihi! What   Er schläft nach der Gassen! Hihi! 's wär'
fun!   fein! –

EVA

I hear a footstep.   Dort hör' ich Schritte.

MAGDALENE
(to Eva)

Come in, now you must.   Jetzt komm', es muss sein!

EVA

Now nearer!   Jetzt näher!

MAGDALENE

You're wrong, there's no-one there.   Du irrst! 's ist nichts, ich wett'.
Now in you come, till your father's in bed. Ei, komm! Du musst, bis der Vater zu Bett.

POGNER
(from inside)

Ho! Lene! Eva!   He! Lene! Eva!

MAGDALENE

'Tis high time!   's ist höchste Zeit!
Listen. Come! It cannot be he!   Hörst du's? Komm'! der Ritter ist weit.

(She pulls the reluctant Eva up the steps to the house.) [16a]

Scene Five. *Walther comes up the alley and turns the corner by Pogner's house. Eva tears herself free from Magdalene and rushes towards him.*

EVA

He's here now!   Da ist er!

MAGDALENE

The time has come to use our wits!   Nun haben wir's! Jetzt heisst's: gescheit!

(She hurries into the house.)

EVA
(overjoyed)

Ah, my true love,   Ja, ihr seid es!
Ah, my own love!   Nein, du bist es!
All I tell thee,   Alles sag' ich,
For thou knowest;   denn ihr wisst es;
All compels me   Alles klag' ich,
And I know it: denn ich weiss es;
You are truly   ihr seid Beides,
Hero, poet,   Held des Preises,
And my only friend!   und mein einz'ger Freund!

WALTHER
(sorrowfully)

Ah, thou art wrong, thy friend am I,   Ach, du irrst! Bin nur dein Freund,
But as poet   doch des Preises

Not yet worthy,	noch nicht würdig,
And the Masters	nicht den Meistern
All do spurn me.	ebenbürtig:
All my passion	mein Begeistern
Met with scorning,	fand Verachten,
And I know it;	und ich weiss es,
Vain my yearning	darf nicht trachten
For my lady's hand.	nach der Freundin Hand!

EVA

Oh how wrong! Her hand alone	Wie du irrst! Der Freundin Hand,
Shall give the victor's prize,	ertheilt nur sie den Preis,
And as thy heart now lives in mine,	wie deinen Muth ihr Herz erfand,
Now shall the crown be thine.	reicht sie nur dir das Reis.

WALTHER

Ah no! Thou art wrong, my lady's hand,	Ach nein! du irrst! Der Freundin Hand,
Though no-one else should gain it	wär' Keinem sie erkoren,
Yet if thy father's will must stand,	wie sie des Vaters Wille band,
Never may I attain it:	mir wär' sie doch verloren.
"A Mastersinger must he be!	[1a] "Ein Meistersinger muss er sein:
He who is crowned and none but he!"	Nur wen ihr krönt, den darf sie frei'n!"
These words your father firmly spake,	So sprach er festlich zu den Herrn,
Though he should wish, he cannot break!	kann nicht zurück, möcht' er's auch gern!
That promise gave me hope;	Das eben gab mir Muth;
And all around me was transformed.	wie ungewohnt mir Alles schien,
I sang, by love inspired,	ich sang mit Lieb' und Gluth,
That I the Master's crown might gain.	dass ich den Meisterschlag verdien'.
But all these Masters!	Doch diese Meister!
Ha! These Masters!	Ha, diese Meister!
All these rhyme-besotted,	Dieser Reim-Gesetze
Old-fashioned poets.	Leimen und Kleister!
With shame and fury	Mir schwillt die Galle,
My heart is fired,	das Herz mir stockt,
Cursing the pitfall	denk' ich der Falle,
To which I was lured.	darein ich gelockt! –
I must seek freedom!	Fort, in die Freiheit!
Back in my own house	Dorthin gehör' ich,
Where I am Master by right.	da wo ich Meister im Haus!
Will you come with me?	Soll ich dich frei'n heut',
I bring you freedom,	dich nun beschwör' ich,
Come and leave here tonight!	flieh', und folg' mir hinaus!
All hope has left me,	Keine Wahl is offen,
Not a choice before me!	nichts steht zu hoffen!
Everywhere Masters	Ueberall Meister,
Like evil creatures,	wie böse Geister,
Round me they're flocking,	seh' ich sich rotten
Jeering and mocking.	mich zu verspotten:
Everywhere judges,	mit den Gewerken,
Markers with grudges	aus den Gemerken,
Out of the alleys	aus allen Ecken,
Making their sallies	auf allen Flecken,
Crowding and hustling,	seh' ich zu Haufen
Masters are bustling;	Meister nur laufen,
Contemptuous faces	mit höhnendem Nicken
Jeering grimaces	frech auf dich blicken,
In circles about you,	in Kreisen und Ringeln
So as to flout you,	dich umzingeln,
Snuffling and screeching,	näselnd und kreischend
Your hand beseeching;	zur Braut dich heischend,
As Masters' plaything	als Meisterbuhle
On the stool they place you,	auf dem Singestuhle,
Trembling and quaking,	zitternd und bebend,
There to disgrace you!	hoch dich erhebend: –
And I must bear it, tamely attend them,	und ich ertrüg' es, sollt' es nicht wagen
Dare not raise a hand to slay them?	grad' aus tüchtig drein zu schlagen?

81

(The nightwatchman's horn sounds. Walther reaches for his sword and stares wildly about him.)

Ha! . . .   Ha! . . .

[25]

EVA
(taking his hand soothingly)

Beloved, waste not your scorn;	Geliebter spare den Zorn!
That was the nightwatchman's horn.	's war nur des Nachtwächters Horn. –
Under the linden	Unter der Linde
Hide yourself quickly,	birg' dich geschwinde:
For here the watchman will pass.	hier kommt der Wächter vorbei.

MAGDALENE
(calls softly)

Eva, now come, it is time.   Evchen! 's ist Zeit: mach' dich frei!

WALTHER

Oh stay!   Du fliehst?

EVA
(smiling)

I must be gone!   Muss ich denn nicht?

WALTHER

But why?   Entweichst?

EVA
(with gentle decision)

The Masters' decree.   Dem Meistergericht.

(She disappears with Magdalene into the house.)

NIGHTWATCHMAN
(appears in the alley. He comes forward singing, turns the corner of Pogner's house and goes off to the left.)

Hark to what I say good people,	"Hört ihr Leut', und lasst euch sagen,
The clock strikes ten in the steeple:	die Glock' hat Zehn geschlagen:
Keep guard now over your fire and light,	bewahrt das Feuer und auch das Licht,
That none may take harm this night.	damit Niemand kein Schad' geschicht!
Praise ye God the Lord!	Lobet Gott den Herrn!"

(He has gone by this time, but his horn is still heard.)

SACHS
(who has been listening behind the door, withdraws the lamp and opens the door a little further.)

[22a]

Now some mischief seems to be planned.	Ueble Dinge, die ich da merk':
Is an abduction near at hand?	[25] eine Entführung gar im Werk!
I watch out! This must not be.	Aufgepasst! das darf nicht sein!

WALTHER
(behind the lime tree)

Will she not come back? Oh what pain!	Käm sie nicht wieder? O der Pein! –
But look, is that she? Ah no!	Doch ja! sie kommt dort! – Weh' mir, nein!
'Tis the older one. Yet surely – yes!	Die Alte ist's! – doch aber – ja!

EVA
(coming out of the house in Magdalene's dress, she hurries towards Walther.)

The foolish child, she's here now, here!   Das thör'ge Kind: da hast du's! da!

(She falls into his arms.)

WALTHER

O Heaven, gazing in your eyes,	O Himmel! Ja! nun wohl ich weiss,
I know I've won the Master-prize!	dass ich gewann den Meisterpreis.

EVA

But no more delaying!	Doch nun kein Besinnen!
Away now! Away now!	Von hinnen! Von hinnen!
If only we were gone!	O wären wir weit schon fort!

WALTHER

Here through the alley,	Hier durch die Gasse: dort
Then ready beyond the gate,	Finden wir vor dem Thor
Squire and horses wait.	Knecht und Rosse vor.

[22a]

(As they both turn to go into the alley, Sachs places his lamp behind a glass globe; a bright beam of light falls across the alley illuminating the lovers.)

EVA
(hastily drawing Walther back)

Alas! The cobbler! If he should see!	O weh', der Schuster! Wenn er uns säh!
Hide now, keep from out of his way!	Birg' dich! komm' ihm nicht in die Näh!

WALTHER

What other way leads to the gate?	Welch' and'rer Weg führt uns hinaus?

[25]

EVA
(pointing right)

Round by the street there; but how it goes,	Dort durch die Strasse: doch der ist kraus,
I'm not sure I know, and there we'd be seen	ich kenn' ihn nicht gut; auch stiessen wir dort
By the watchman.	auf den Wächter.

WALTHER

So then, through the alley!	Nun denn: durch die Gasse!

EVA

But we must wait till the cobbler goes.	Der Schuster muss erst vom Fenster fort.

WALTHER

I'll make him turn from his window.	Ich zwing' ihn, dass er's verlasse.

EVA

Keep out of sight, he knows you.	Zeig' dich ihm nicht: er kennt dich!

WALTHER

The cobbler?	Der Schuster?

EVA

'Tis Sachs!	's ist Sachs!

WALTHER

Hans Sachs? My friend?	Hans Sachs? Mein Freund?

EVA

Not so!	Glaub's nicht!
For he speaks of you only to flout you.	Von dir zu sagen Uebles nur wusst' er.

WALTHER

What? Sachs? He too? I'll put out his light!	Wie, Sachs? Auch er? – Ich lösch' ihm das Licht!

EVA
(restraining Walther)

No, no! – But hark!	Thu's nicht! – Doch horch!

(Beckmesser has come up the alley, slinking behind the nightwatchman. He peers up at the windows of Pogner's house and, leaning against Sachs's house, stands up on the stone seat. He begins to tune a lute.)

WALTHER

That's a lute I hear.   Einer Laute Klang'?

EVA

Ah! My distress!   Ach meine Noth!

(*As Sachs hears the first sounds of the lute a thought strikes him; he turns down his light and opens the lower part of the door.*)

WALTHER

What do you fear?   Wie, wird dir bang?
The cobbler, see, has moved his light: Der Schuster, sieh, zog ein das Licht: –
Now let us go!   so sei's gewagt!

EVA

Ah! See you not there?   Weh'! Hörst du denn nicht?
Another comes and takes his stand.   Ein And'rer kam, und nahm dort stand.

WALTHER

I hear and see: – he has a lute.   Ich hör's und seh's: – ein Musikant.
But why's he here so late at night?   Was will der hier so spät des Nachts?

EVA
(*in despair*)

'Tis Beckmesser, ah!   's ist Beckmesser schon!

SACHS
(*unseen, has placed his workbench in the doorway; he overhears Eva's cry.*)

So I was right!   Aha! Ich dacht's!

WALTHER

The Marker? He? And here in my power?   Der Merker! Er? in meiner Gewalt?
Then on! He'll get what he deserves.   D'rauf zu! den Lung'rer mach' ich kalt!

EVA

Now God forbid! Would you awake my   Um Gott! So hör! Willst den Vater wecken?
father?
He'll sing a song, and then he'll go.   Er singt ein Lied, dann zieht er ab.
Come, let us hide within this arbour!   Lass' dort uns in Gebüsch verstecken. –
Ah, me, what trouble with men I have!   Was mit den Männern ich Müh' doch hab'!

(*She draws Walther onto the seat behind the bushes under the lime tree. Beckmesser strums loudly on the lute, gazing eagerly at the window and waiting for it to open. When he is about to sing, Sachs strikes a heavy blow on the last, turns the light of his lamp full on the street again, and himself sings loudly.*)

SACHS

Jerum! Jerum!   [11, 29]   Jerum! Jerum!
   Halla halla he!   Halla halla he!
Oho! Trallalei! O he!   Oho! Trallalei! O he!
When Eve from Paradise was cast,   Als Eva aus dem Paradies
   Her sin she soon repented,   von Gott dem Herrn verstossen,
For, limping o'er the stony path,   gar shuf ihr Schmerz der harte Kies
   Her feet were sore tormented.   an ihrem Fuss, dem blossen.
That filled the Lord with woe,   Das jammerte den Herrn,
   Her feet he cherished so,   ihr Füsschen hat er gern,
And then an angel did he choose   und seinem Engel rief er zu:
To make for her a pair of shoes,   "da mach' der armen Sünd'rin Schuh'!
And since poor Adam, as I know,   Und da der Adam, wie ich seh',
Against the stones had stubbed his toe,   an Steinen dort sich stösst die Zeh',
   To help him walk   dass recht fortan
   Without a care,   er wandeln kann,
Made for him another pair!   so miss' dem auch Stiefeln an!"

WALTHER
(*to Eva*)

What can he mean? He sings your name.   Wie heisst das Lied? Wie nennt er dich?

EVA
(whispering to Walther)

I also heard: it is not I;	Ich hört' es schon: 's geht nicht auf mich.
Yet hidden malice I can hear.	Doch eine Bosheit steckt darin.

WALTHER

Why must we stay? The time goes by!	Welch Zögerniss! Die Zeit geht hin!

BECKMESSER
(jumps up angrily from the seat and sees Sachs at work.)

What can that be?	Was soll das sein? –
Accursed noise!	Verdammtes Schrein!
What's on that stupid cobbler's mind?	Was fällt dem groben Schuster ein?

(comes up to Sachs)

What? Master? Up? And so late at night?	Wie, Meister? Auf? So spät zur Nacht?

SACHS

Why Beckmesser, not asleep?	Herr Stadtschreiber! Was, ihr wacht? –
Your shoes cause you a needless worry!	Die Schuh' machen euch grosse Sorgen?
You see they'll be done, if I but hurry!	Ihr seht, ich bin dran: ihr habt sie morgen.

(He works.)

BECKMESSER

Give the devil the shoes!	Hol' der Teufel die Schuh'!
Here I want peace!	Ich will hier Ruh'!

SACHS
(working)

Jerum! Jerum!	Jerum! Jerum!
Halla halla he!	Halla halla he!
Oho! Trallalei! O he!	Oho! Trallalei! O he!
Oh Eve, for shame you now should weep,	O Eva! Eva! Schlimmes Weib!
For this is all your doing,	Das hast du am Gewissen,
That now the feet of mortal men	dass ob der Füss' am Menschenleib
The angels must be shoeing!	jetzt Engel schustern müssen.
Had you left fruit alone	Bliebst du im Paradies,
You ne'er had trod on stone.	da gab es keinen Kies.
Because you followed your giddy head	Ob deiner jungen Missethat
I now sit here with awl and thread,	handthier' ich jetzt mit Ahl' und Draht,
And Adam listened to that witch,	und ob Herrn Adam's übler Schwäch'
That's why I'm soling shoes with pitch!	versohl' ich Schuh' und streiche Pech.
And were not I	Wär' ich nicht fein
An angel too	ein Engel rein,
Devils might make shoes for you!	Teufel möchte Schuster sein!

WALTHER
(to Eva)

We or the Marker?	Uns, oder dem Marker?
At whom does he jeer?	Wem spielt er den Streich?

EVA
(to Walther)

His song reproves	Ich fürcht', uns dreien
All three, I fear.	gilt es gleich.
Ah woe is me!	O weh, der Pein!
I fear some evil.	Mir ahnt nichts Gutes!

WALTHER

My sweetest angel,	Mein süsser Engel,
Be of good courage!	sei guten Muthes!

EVA

'Tis the song that wounds.	Mich betrübt das Lied!

WALTHER

I hear it not;	Ich hör es kaum!
Thou art by me:	Du bist bei mir:
What blissful dream!	Welch' holder Traum!

(*He draws Eva tenderly to him.*)

BECKMESSER
(*threateningly to Sachs*)

Stop it at once!	Gleich höret auf!
Is this a trick?	Spielt ihr mir Streich'?
Don't you know	Bleibt ihr Tag's
The day from night?	Und Nacht's euch gleich!

SACHS

If here I sing,	Wenn ich hier sing',
What's that to you?	was kümmert's euch?
And mind you! Shoes	Die Schuhe sollen
You will need tomorrow!	doch fertig werden?

BECKMESSER

Then go inside	So schliesst euch ein
And leave me in peace.	Und schweigt dazu still!

SACHS

But night shoemaking	Des Nachts arbeiten
Brings much sorrow;	macht Beschwerden;
If I'm to drive	Wenn ich da munter
Away dull care,	bleiben will,
I need fresh air	da brauch' ich Luft
And cheerful song;	und frischen Gesang;
So now for the third verse!	drum hört wie der dritte
'Tis not long!	Vers gelang!

(*He waxes his thread carefully.*)

BECKMESSER

He drives me frantic! This infamous noise!	Er macht mich rasend! – Das grobe Geschrei!
Oh God, she will think 'tis I who sing!	Am End' denkt sie gar, dass ich das sei!

(*Beckmesser stops his ears and walks in despair up and down the alley*.)

SACHS
(*working*)

Jerum! Jerum!	Jerum! Jerum!
Halla halla he!	Halla halla he!
Oho! Trallalei! O he!	Oho! Trallalei! O he!
O Eva hear my tale of woe [32]	O Eva! Hör' mein Klageruf,
And let us mourn together!	mein Noth und schwer Verdrüssen!
The world condemns the cobbler's soul	Die Kunstwerk', die ein Schuster schuf,
And tramples on his leather!	sie tritt die Welt mit Füssen!
Without an angel there,	Gäb nicht ein Engel Trost,
To drive away my care,	der gleiches Werk erlos't,
And call me up to Paradise,	und rief' mich oft in's Paradies,
I'd leave this work that I despise!	wie dann ich Schuh' und Stiefel liess'!
But when enthroned in Heaven on high	Doch wenn der mich im Himmel hält,
The world beneath my feet will lie,	dann liegt zu Füssen mir die Welt,
Then, born anew,	und bin in Ruh'
I am a shoe–	Hans Sachs ein Schuh–
Maker and a poet too!	macher und Poet dazu.

BECKMESSER

The window is opening: Good Lord! 'Tis she!	Das Fenster geht auf: – Herr Gott, 's ist sie!

(*Magdalene, in Eva's dress, cautiously opens the window and looks out.*)

EVA
(to Walther, in great agitation)

His song so pains me, I know not why!	Mich schmerzt das Lied, ich weiss nicht wie!
Away let us hasten!	O fort, lass' uns fliehen!

WALTHER
(impetuously)

Yes, now! with my sword.	Nun denn: mit dem Schwert!

EVA

Not that! Ah no!	Nicht doch! Ach halt'!

WALTHER
(taking his hand from his sword)

Scarce worth the while.	Kaum wär er's werth!

EVA

Yes, patience is best! O best of men!	Ja, besser Geduld! O lieber Mann!
That I should cause you so much pain.	Dass ich so Noth dir machen kann!

BECKMESSER

Now if he sings longer I shall be lost.	Jetzt bin ich verloren, singt der noch fort! –

(He comes up to Sachs and stands with his back to the alley, playing his lute so as to hold Magdalene's attention.)

WALTHER
(softly to Eva)

Who's at the window?	Wer ist am Fenster?

EVA
(softly)

'Tis Magdalene.	's ist Magdalene.

WALTHER

That's turning the tables! I can't help laughing.	Das heiss' ich vergelten! fast muss ich lachen.

EVA

Oh, how I long to end all this trouble!	Wie ich ein End' und Flucht mir ersehne!

WALTHER

If only he would begin his story.	Ich wünscht' er möchte den Anfang machen.

(Walther and Eva, leaning tenderly together on the seat, follow the scene between Sachs and Beckmesser with growing interest.)

BECKMESSER

Friend Sachs! Let me but speak a word!	Freund Sachs! So hört doch nur ein Wort!
Why let the shoes so much distress you?	Wie seid ihr auf die Schuh' versessen!
I give my word I'd clean forgotten them.	Ich hatt' sie wahrlich schon vergessen!
As shoemaker I know your worth,	Als Schuster seid ihr mir wohl werth,
In art your place is first on earth.	als Kunstfreund doch weit mehr verehrt.
Your judgement, too, is seldom wrong;	Eu'r Urtheil, glaubt, das halt ich hoch;
I beg you, hear this little song;	drum bitt' ich: hört das Liedlein doch,
For, help from you I'd gladly borrow,	mit dem ich morgen möcht' gewinnen,
That I may win the prize tomorrow.	ob das auch recht nach euren Sinnen.

SACHS
(as before)

Aha! Flattery will not hold me!	O ha! Wollt mich beim Wahne fassen?
Never again will I let you scold me.	Mag mich nicht wieder schelten lassen.
For since your cobbler took to verse	Seit sich der Schuster dünkt Poet,
The shoes he makes have grown worse and worse;	gar übel es um eu'r Schuhwerk steht;
Unsound throughout,	ich seh' wie's schlappt,
They flap all about!	und überall klappt:

Therefore on verse and rhyme,	drum lass' ich Vers' und Reim'
No more I'll waste my time,	gar billig nun daheim,
My skill, my wit, no longer I'll use	Verstand und Kenntniss auch dazu,
So that tomorrow you'll have your shoes!	mach' euch für morgen die neuen Schuh'.

BECKMESSER
(shrieking as he strums his lute)

No, let that be! 'Twas only my jest,	Lasst das doch sein! das war ja nur Scherz.
My true feelings you might have guessed.	Vernehmt besser, wie's mir um's Herz!
The folk think well of you	Vom Volk seid ihr geehrt,
And the maiden esteems you too:	Auch der Pognerin seid ihr werth:
When for tomorrow's Prize	will ich vor aller Welt
I sing to win her favour,	nun morgen um die werben,
In vain, I would endeavour,	sagt, könnt's mich nicht verderben,
If my song she should despise.	wenn mein Lied euch nicht gefällt?
So listen now to me	Drum hört mich ruhig an;
And tell me honestly,	und sang ich, sagt mir dann,
Where it is right and wrong,	was euch gefällt, was nicht,
And I'll improve my song!	dass ich mich danach richt'.

(He strums his lute again.)

SACHS

Oh that could never be;	Ei lasst mich doch in Ruh'!
How could such honour fall to me?	Wie käm' solche Ehr' mir zu?
If nought but doggerel rhymes I can stammer	Nur Gassenhauer dicht' ich zum meisten:
Then doggerel I sing as my leather I hammer.	drum sing' ich zur Gassen, und hau' auf den Leisten.

(working)

Jerum! Jerum!	Jerum! Jerum!
Halla halla hei!	Halla halla hei!

BECKMESSER

Accursed rogue! All my senses leave me,	Verfluchter Kerl! – Den Verstand verlier' ich,
Amid his song that reeks of blacking!	mit seinem Lied von Pech und Schmierich! –
Silence! You'll wake the neighbours up!	Schweigt doch! Weckt ihr die Nachbarn auf?

SACHS

They're used to it, they will not stir.	Die sind's gewohnt: 's hört Keiner drauf. –
"O Eva, Eva!"	"O Eva! Eva!" –

BECKMESSER
(furious)

Oh you base, black-hearted rascal!	O ihr boshafter Geselle!
More tricks like this you'll not play here!	Ihr spielt mir heut' den letzten Streich!
Now at once, stop all that howling,	Schweight ihr nicht auf der Stelle,
Or you'll repent your trick I swear!	so denkt ihr dran, das schwör' ich euch.
You are always so envious:	Neidisch seid ihr, nichts weiter,
Though you think yourself so clever,	dünkt ihr euch gleich gescheiter:
That other men have wits always enraged you:	dass Andre auch 'was sind, ärgert euch schändlich!
But I know you well and can see through you!	Glaubt, ich kenne euch aus – und innwendlich!
That you cannot play the Marker's part,	Dass man euch noch nicht zum Merker gewählt,
So grieves your cantankerous cobbler's heart.	das ist's, was den gallichten Schuster quält.
Ah well, so long as Beckmesser sings;	[22a] Nun gut! So lang' als Beckmesser lebt,
While a single rhyme to his lips he brings;	und ihm noch ein Reim an den Lippen klebt,
So long as I among Masters am famed,	so lang' ich noch bei den Meistern was gelt',
Though Nuremberg bloom and wax,	ob Nürnberg "blüh' oder wachs'"
I swear to you Hans Sachs,	das schwör ich Herrn Hans Sachs:
Never shall you as Marker be named.	nie wird er je zum Merker bestellt!

(He strums in intense fury.)

SACHS
(who has listened to him quietly)

Was that your song?	War das eu'r Lied?

BECKMESSER

The devil take it!	Der Teufel hol's!

SACHS

The rules were lacking, but brave the sound.	Zwar wenig Regel: doch klang's recht stolz!

BECKMESSER

Will you not listen?	Wollt ihr mich hören?

SACHS

For Heaven's sake, then, Sing on, while soles for your shoes I'm making.	In Gottes Namen, singt zu: ich schlag' auf die Sohl' die Rahmen.

BECKMESSER

But, you'll keep quiet?	Doch schweigt ihr still?

SACHS

Oh, please sing on, My cobbling, look, is not yet done.	Ei, singet ihr, die Arbeit, schaut, fördert's auch mir.

(He continues working.)

BECKMESSER

That accursed knocking passes all bearing.	Das verfluchte Klopfen wollt ihr doch lassen?

SACHS

How else can your shoes be fit for wearing?	Wie sollt' ich die Sohl' euch richtig fassen?

BECKMESSER

How can I sing though through so much clamour?	Was? wollt ihr klopfen, und ich soll singen?

SACHS

Yours is the song, mine the shoe and hammer.	Euch muss da Lied, mir der Schuh' gelingen.

BECKMESSER

I don't want the shoes!	Ich mag keine Schuh'!

SACHS

That's where you're wrong, For tomorrow you'll sing a different song.	Das sagt ihr jetzt; in der Singschul' ihr mir's dann wieder versetzt. –
But wait! Perhaps it can be done; As partners we can work as one. Though to your shoes I must keep turning The Art of Marker I would be learning.	Doch hört! Vielleicht sich's richten lässt: zwei-einig geht der Mensch zu best. Darf ich die Arbeit nicht entfernen, die Kunst des Merkers möcht' ich doch lernen:
In that you have no peer, it's true: How could I learn, if not from you? So sing away, and I will mark And still make progress with my work.	darin nun kommt euch Keiner gleich; ich lern' sie nie, wenn nicht von euch. Drum singt ihr nun, ich acht' und merk', und fördr' auch wohl dabei mein Werk.

BECKMESSER

Mark for me, then, and if I go wrong, Score with your chalk as I sing my song.	Merkt immer zu; und was nicht gewann, nehmt eure Kreide, und streicht mir's an.

SACHS

No sir! With chalk can no shoes be nailed. With my hammer on the last I'll mark where you've failed.	Nein, Herr! da fleckten die Schuh' mir nicht: mit dem Hammer auf den Leisten halt' ich Gericht.

BECKMESSER

Accursed malice! God, now it's late!

I must strike up soon or the maid won't wait!

Verdammte Bosheit! – Gott, und's wird spät!
am End' mir die Jungfer vom Fenster geht!

(He strums eagerly.)

SACHS
(with a blow of his hammer)

Now begin, time flies: or I'll sing again.

Fanget an! 's pressiert! Sonst sing' ich für mich!

BECKMESSER

No, not that! Be silent! Devil! How troublesome!
Now if you're going to mark, you must watch me.
That's right! Just strike with the hammer when you catch me:
But you must abide by the rules alone;

Do not mark phrases the rules may allow.

Haltet ein! nur das nicht! – Teufel! wie ägerlich! –
Wollt ihr euch denn als Merker erdreisten,
nun gut, so merkt mit dem Hammer auf den Leisten: –
nur mit dem Beding, nach den Regeln scharf;
aber nichts, was nach den Regeln ich darf.

SACHS

On the cobblers' rules then I take my stand,
Who has work that's burning beneath his hand.

Nach den Regeln, wie sie der Schuster kennt,
dem die Arbeit unter den Händen brennt.

BECKMESSER

By Masters' rule?

Auf Meister-Ehr'!

SACHS

And cobbler's tool!

Und Schuster-Muth!

BECKMESSER

Never a fault then, fair and good!

Nicht einen Fehler: glatt und gut!

SACHS

Then you tomorrow go unshoed.
Sit you down here!

Dann gingt ihr morgen unbeschuh't. –
Setzt euch denn hier!

(pointing to the stone seat at the shop door)

BECKMESSER
(draws back to the corner of the house.)

I'd rather stand here.

Lasst hier mich stehen!

SACHS

But why so far?

Warum so fern?

BECKMESSER

Because the Marker
Must not be seen; so says the rule.

Euch nicht zu sehen,
wie's Brauch in der Schul' vor dem Gemerk'.

SACHS

Then I shall not hear.

Da hör' ich euch schlecht.

BECKMESSER

My voice is full;
More sweetly to your ear 'twill sound.

Der Stimme Stärk'
ich so gar lieblich dämpfen kann.

WALTHER
(softly to Eva)

Are we all mad, or in a dream?

I'm still there in the school it seems.

[25] Welch' toller Spuck! Mich dünkt's ein Traum:
den Singstuhl, scheint's, verliess ich kaum!

EVA
(resting her head on Walther's breast)

Sweet sleep enfolds me like a spell:　　Die Schläf' umwebt mir's, wie ein Wahn:
For good or evil, who can tell?　　ob's Heil, ob Unheil, was ich ahn'?

(Beckmesser takes up position around the corner, opposite the window.)

SACHS

How fine! – I'm ready! Now begin!　　Wie fein! – Nun gut denn! – Fanget an!

(Beckmesser tunes down the D string – which he has unconsciously screwed up in his rage – Magdalene leans out of the window.)

BECKMESSER
(playing his lute)

"I see now dawning daylight,　　[30]　　"Den Tag seh' ich erscheinen,
That gives me delight true . . ."　　der mir wohl gefall'n thut . . ."

(Sachs strikes his hammer. Beckmesser starts but continues.)

"And wakes in me a gay, light　　"Da fasst mein Herz sich einen
Heart and a courage . . ."　　guten und frischen Muth."

(Sachs has dealt two blows. Beckmesser turns round and asks in an angry undertone.)

Is that a joke?　　Treibt ihr hier Scherz?
What fault can you find there?　　Was wär' nicht gelungen?

SACHS

Better have sung there:　　Desser gesungen:
"And wakes in me　　"da fasst mein Herz
A gay, light heart and courage."　　sich einen guten und frischen Muth."

BECKMESSER

Pray how would it rhyme then　　Wie sollt' sich das reimen
With "now dawning daylight"?　　auf "seh' ich erscheinen"?

SACHS

Is accent to you so small a matter?　　Ist euch an der Weise nichts gelegen?
I think the phrase should fit the rhyme!　　Mich dünkt, 'sollt' passen Ton und Wort.

BECKMESSER

I will not argue! Stop all that clatter,　　Mit euch zu streiten?–Lässt von den Schlägen,

Or you will repent!　　sonst denkt ihr mir dran!

SACHS

You're wasting time.　　　　　　Jetzt fahret fort!

BECKMESSER

I'm all upset!　　Bin ganz verwirrt!

SACHS

　　Begin it once more:　　　　　So fangt noch 'mal an:
Three faults I pass as marked before.　　drei Schläg' ich jetzt pausieren kann.

BECKMESSER
(aside)

I'll take no notice of what he may say,　　Am Besten, wenn ich ihn gar nicht beacht': –
As long as she likes the way I play!　　wenn's nur die Jungfer nicht irre macht!
(He clears his throat and begins again.)
"I see now dawning daylight,　　[30]　　"Den Tag seh' ich erscheinen,
That gives me delight true;　　der mir wohl gefallen thut;
And wakes in me a gay, light　　da fasst mein Herz sich einen
Heart and a courage new.　　guten und frischen Muth.
I think not now of dying;　　Da denk' ich nicht an Sterben,
　　Rather of trying　　　　lieber an Werben
A young maiden to win.　　um jung Mägdeleins Hand.
Why think I of this day,　　Warum wohl aller Tage
It other days doth excel?　　schönster mag dieser sein?
Loudly to all I say it,　　Allen ich hier es sage:

91

That I love a damsel	weil ein schönes Fräulein
Whose father gives me truly,	von ihrem lieb'n Herrn Vater,
Promises duly,	wie gelobt hat er,
I as bridegroom shall stand.	ist bestimmt zum Eh'stand.
Let all who dare	Wer sich getrau',
Now come and stare	der komm' und schau'
Here upon the maiden so fair,	da steh'n die hold lieblich Jungfrau,
With whom I fondly hope to pair	auf die ich all' mein' Hoffnung bau';
Therefore seemeth brighter the air	darum ist der Tag so schön blau,
Today in all the land."	als ich anfänglich fand."

(From the sixth line onwards Sachs makes repeated blows with his hammer; Beckmesser starts at each blow and, trying to contain his anger, he sings in abrupt phrases to comic effect. Finally he angrily confronts Sachs.)

BECKMESSER

Sachs! Sachs! You drive me mad!	Sachs! – Seht! – Ihr bringt mich um!
Will you keep quiet?	Wollt ihr jetzt schweigen?

SACHS

No word I've said!	Ich bin ja stumm?
I'm only marking. We'll talk anon.	Die Zeichen merkt' ich: wir sprechen dann;
Meanwhile, soling your shoes will go on.	derweil' lassen die Sohlen sich an.

BECKMESSER
(seeing that Magdalene is going to withdraw from the window)

She is going. Bst! Bst! I must be quick!	Sie entweicht? Bst! Bst! – Herr Gott! Ich muss!

(shaking his fist at Sachs)

Sachs, I'll remember this spiteful trick.	Sachs! Euch gedenk' ich die Aergernuss!

(He prepares for the second verse.)

SACHS
(brandishing his hammer)

Marker at hand:	Merker am Ort!
Take your stand!	Fahret fort!

BECKMESSER
(getting louder and more breathless)

"This morning my heart light is,	"Will heut' mir das Herz hüpfen,
When I her look upon:	werben um Fräulein jung,
Her father, as his right is,	doch thät der Vater knüpfen
Makes one condition,	daran ein' Bedingung
For him who would his heir be,	für den, wer ihn beerben
And eke the pair be	will, und auch werben
Of his daughter so sweet,	um sein Kindelein fein.
His daughter he well loveth,	Der Zunft ein bied'rer Meister
A Master renowned here,	wohl sein' Tochter er liebt,
And at the same time proveth	doch zugleich auch beweist er,
That to him Art is dear:	was er auf die Kunst giebt:
The prize first must he bring her,	zum Preise muss es bringen
As Mastersinger,	im Meistersinger,
Who'd be a wooer fit.	wer sein Eidam will sein.
Now art is, quoth	Nun gilt es Kunst
He, what here go'th	dass mit Vergunst
Free from common and empty froth	ohn' all' schädlich gemeinen Dunst,
As prize-man must he plight his troth,	ihm glücke des Preises Gewunst,
Who desires, with a heart unloth	wer begehrt mit wahrer Inbrunst
As spouse the maid to greet!"	um die Jungfrau zu frein."

(Beckmesser, his eyes fixed on the window, has been increasingly alarmed by Magdalene's obvious dissatisfaction; he sings louder and quicker to drown Sachs's hammering. Sachs shakes his head and gives up marking the separate faults but hammers on to finish the shoe. Beckmesser is about to continue when Sachs withdraws the shoes, rises from his stool and leans out over the shop door.)

Say, have you finished?   Seid ihr nun fertig?

BECKMESSER
(*in anguish*)

   Why ask you now?   Wie fraget ihr?

SACHS
(*He triumphantly holds out the completed shoes.*)

Since the shoes are both quite ready now.	Mit den Schuhen ward ich fertig schier! –
I call that a proper Marker's shoe!	Das heiss' ich mir rechte Merkerschuh': –
My Marker's poem's finished too!	mein Merkersprüchlein hört dazu!

(*He waves the shoes about in the air by the laces*)

By long and short strokes beaten,	Mit lang' und kurzen Hieben,
Upon your sole 'tis written:	steht's auf der Sohl' geschrieben:
Now read it well	da les't es klar
And what it tells	und nehmt es wahr,
Remember ever more.	und merkt's euch immerdar:
Good song keeps time;	Gut Lied will Takt,
And proper rhyme,	wer den verzwackt,
And lest your pen forget it,	dem Schreiber mit der Feder
Upon your shoes I have set it.	haut ihn der Schuster auf's Leder. –
Now take your road,	Nun lauft in Ruh',
You're rightly shod:	habt gute Schuh';
These shoes will fit your feet;	der Fuss euch drin nicht knackt;
Their soles will mark the beat!	ihn hält die Sohl' im Takt!

(*He laughs loudly.*)

BECKMESSER
(*has retreated into the alley; with his back to the wall, he shakes his lute at Sachs while he yells his third verse in a breathless hurry at the top of his voice.*)

"That I Master was duly	"Darf ich Meister mich nennen,
Chosen, I'd show to her;	das bewähr' ich heut' gern,
To win the prize I truly	weil nach dem Preis ich brenne
Burn with thirst and hunger.	muss dursten und hungern.
The nine Muses I summon,	Nun ruf' ich die neun Musen,
That they may come on,	dass an sie blusen
And my attainments prove.	mein dicht' rischen Verstand.
I've kept the rules exactly,	Wohl kenn' ich alle Regeln,
Measure and beat I know;	halte gut Maass und Zahl;
And, if my song goes roundly,	doch Sprung und Ueberkegeln
Some slips maybe let go,	wohl passirt je einmal,
If with heart full of terrors,	wann der Kopf, ganz voll Zagen,
He make some errors	zu frei'n will wagen
Who seeks for a maid's love.	um ein' jung Mägdleins Hand.
For, by the Muse,	Ein Junggesell,
My skin I'd lose,	trug ich mein Fell,
My office, rank, the goods I use,	mein Ehr', Amt, Würd', und Brod zur Stell',
That you the prize should not refuse,	dass euch mein Gesang wohl gefäll',
And me the young damsel should choose,	und mich das Jungfräulein erwähl',
If she my song approve."	wann sie mein Lied gut fand."

NEIGHBOURS
(*One by one, they open the windows in the alley and look out.*)

Who's howling there? Who cries so loud?	Wer heult denn da? Wer kreischt mit Macht?
So late at night, is that allowed?	Ist das erlaubt so spät zur Nacht? –
Keep quiet there! It's time for bed!	Gebt ruhe hier! 's ist Schlafenszeit! –
That donkey's bray would wake the dead!	Nein, hört nur, wie der Esel schreit! –
You there! Be still! And get you gone!	Ihr da! Seid still, und scheert euch fort!
Go howling in some other place!	Heult, kreischt und schreit an and'rem Ort!

DAVID
(*peering out of the window*)

Who ever's this? – And who's up there?	Wer Teufel hier – Und drüben gar?

(*He recognises Magdalene.*)

That's Lene there, it's her I'm sure.   Die Lene ist's, – ich seh' es klar!
Good Lord, 'twas he! She told him to come.   Herr Je! das war's, den hat sie bestellt;
This then is the fellow that she prefers.   der ist's, der ihr besser als ich gefällt! –
Wait till I begin! I'll polish your skin!   Nun warte! du kriegst's! dir streich' ich das Fell!

(He goes in and returns with a cudgel. Magdalene, seeing him, makes urgent signs to him to go away. Beckmesser interprets these as signs of displeasure; his singing expresses his despair.)

Scene Seven. *David climbs out of the window, throws himself on Beckmesser and holds him firmly by the collar while he struggles to escape.*

DAVID

The devil take your song, you cursed rogue!   Zum Teufel mit der verdammter Gesell'!

(He knocks Beckmesser's lute out of his hands.)

MAGDALENE
(cries from the window)

Oh Heaven! David! Lord, what ill luck!   Ach Himmel! David! Gott, welche Noth!
Oh stop them! Oh stop them! They both will be dead!   Zu Hülfe! zu Hülfe! Sie schlagen sich todt!

(More and more Prentices come from all sides.)

BECKMESSER
(struggling with David)

Accursed knave! Let me go free!   Verfluchter Kerl! Lässt du mich los?

DAVID

Not yet, I'll thrash you till you can't stand!   Gewiss! Die Glieder brech' ich dir blos!

(They continue to struggle and fight.)

NEIGHBOURS
(at their windows)

Look out! Come on! Two men are fighting there!   Seht nach! Springt zu! Da würgen sich zwei!

(David and Beckmesser wrestle. They roll about the stage fighting. Beckmesser attempts to escape, but David catches and beats him.)

NEIGHBOURS
(coming down into the street)

Halloa! Come on! There's fighting here: Heda! Herbei! 's giebt Prügelei!
You there, let go! Now let him go!   Ihr da! aus einander! Gebt freien lauf!
Let go your hold or we'll fight too!   Lasst ihr nicht los, wir schlagen drauf!

1ST NEIGHBOUR

What now? What you here? What's that to you?   Ei seht! Aus ihr da? Geht's euch was' an?

2ND NEIGHBOUR

What seek you here? What have they done to you?   Was sucht ihr hier? Hat man euch 'was gethan?

1ST NEIGHBOUR

All know you well!   Euch kennt man gut!

2ND NEIGHBOUR

They know you better!   Euch noch viel besser!

1ST NEIGHBOUR

How so, then?   Wie so denn?

2ND NEIGHBOUR
(He strikes him.)

Well, so!   Ei, so!

MAGDALENE

David! Beckmesser!   David! Beckmesser!

PRENTICES
(*entering*)

Come on! Come on! They're fighting here!   Herbei! Herbei! 's gibt Keilerei!

1ST PRENTICES

'Tis the cobblers!   's sind die Schuster!

2ND PRENTICES

No, 'tis the tailors!   Nein, 's sind die Schneider!

1ST PRENTICES

The drunken wretches!   Die Trunkenbolde!

2ND PRENTICES

Starving beggars!   Die Hungerleider!

NEIGHBOURS
(*to one another*)

That long have I owed you! –	Euch gönnt' ich's schon lange! –
Are you afraid then?	Wird euch wohl bange?
That for the payment! –	Das für die Klage! –
Have a care if I strike you!	Seht euch vor, wenn ich schlage!
What! Has your wife been cross? –	Hat euch die Frau gehetzt? –
See how the cudgel falls!	Schau' wie es Prügel setzt! –
What, not yet found your wits? –	Seid ihr noch nicht gewitzt? –
You still strike! – Take that!	So schlagt doch! – Das sitzt! –
What you, you scoundrel?	Dass dich, Hallunke! –
Just let me catch you!	Hie Färbertunke! –
Wait there you rascal!	Wartet, ihr Racker!
Short weight swindlers!	Ihr Maasabzwacker! –
Donkey! Stupid!	Esel! Dummrian! –
Stupid!	Du Grobian! –
Blockhead!	Lümmel du! –
Never waver!	Drauf und zu!

PRENTICES
(*to one another*)

We know the locksmiths,	Kennt man die Schlosser nicht?
Surely they're the ones who started this.	Die haben's sicher angericht'! –
I'm sure the smiths have started this.	Ich glaub' die Schmiede werden's sein, –
I know the joiners there!	Die Schreiner seh' ich dort beim Schein,
Hey! See the coopers in the dance!	Hei! Schau' die Schäffler dort beim Tanz. –
I know the barbers at a glance;	Dort seh' die Bader ich im Glanz. –
Grocers too, a timid band,	Krämer finden sich zur Hand;
With barleysugar sticks in hand,	mit Gerstenstang und Zuckerkand;
With peppercorns and cinnamon!	mit Pfeffer, Zimmt, Muscatennuss,
They smell alright,	Sie riechen schön,
They smell alright,	Sie riechen schön,
But spoil the appetite,	doch haben viel Verdruss,
And hesitate to fight.	und blieben gern vom Schuss. –
See that fool there,	Seht nur, der Hase
With his nose everywhere! –	Hat üb'rall die Nase! –
Do you wish to speak to me? –	Meinst du damit etwa mich? –
Am I meant to speak to you? –	Mein' ich damit etwa dich? –
There's one nose I've pounded! –	Du hast's auf die Schnautze! –
Lord! How that sounded! –	Herr, jetzt setzt's Plautze! –
Ha! There goes! Crack! Like a thunderclap!	Hei! Krach! Hagelwetterschlag!
Where that fell, the hair won't grow so soon!	Wo das sitzt, da wächst nichts nach!
Fight ye bravely!	Keilt euch wacker,
Never waver!	Hau't die Racker!
Hold your own though journeymen should come!	Haltet selbst Gesellen Stand;
If you give way, 'twould be a shame!	wer da wich', 's wär' wahrlich Schand'!

95

Now merrily lay on!
Like one man
Stand we all, and fight with might and main!

Drauf und dran!
Wie ein Mann
steh'n wir alle zur Keilerei!

JOURNEYMEN
(hurrying on from different sides)

Hey, all you fellows there!
The sound of strife and blows I hear.
Come on, there's fighting close at hand;
All journeymen, come take your stand!
'Tis the weavers! 'Tis the tanners!
'Tis then as I thought!
The bargain-spoilers!
Always at their games!
There the butcher Klaus
Plainly I see!
Guilds! Guilds!
Guilds come along!
Tailors with their measures!
Hey there go their cudgels!
Girdlers! – Pewterers! –
Glue-boilers! – Wax-boilers!
Cloth-cutters here!
Flaxweavers!
Come here! Come here!
Come along if you dare!
Now gaily let us go and join the fray!
We get here just in time!
Run home, you'll catch it from your wife!
Here you'll get painted black and blue!
    Come along!
    Come along!
    Give it him!
Comrades, Guilds, come along!

Heda! Gesellen 'ran!
Dort wird mit Streit und Zank gethan.
Da giebt's gewiss gleich Schlägerei;
Gesellen, haltet euch dabei!
'Sind die Weber und Gerber! –
Dacht' ich's doch gleich! –
Die Preisverderber!
Spielen immer Streich'! –
Dort den Metzger Klaus
den kennt man heraus!
Zünfte! Zünfte!
Zünfte heraus! –
Schneider mit dem Bügel!
Hei! hie setzt's Prügel!
Gürtler! – Zinngiesser! –
Leimsieder! – Lichtgiesser! –
Tuchscherer her!
Leinweber!
Hieher! Hieher!
Immer mehr! Immer mehr!
Nur tüchtig drauf! Wir schlagen los:
jetzt wird die Keilerei erst gross! –
Lauft heim, sonnst kriegt ihr's von der Frau;
hier giebt's nur Prügel-Färbeblau!
    Immer 'ran!
    Man für Mann!
    Schlagt sie nieder!
Zünfte! Zünfte! Heraus! –

MASTERS
(The Masters and older citizens arrive from different sides.)

What is this sound of brawl and strife?
It sounds from near and far!
Now each of you must hurry home at once to bed,
Or blows will rain like hailstones on your heads!
Do not crowd together there,
Otherwise we'll join the fray!

Was giebt's denn da für Zank und Streit?
Das tos't ja weit und breit!
Gebt Ruh' und scheer' sich jeder heim,
sonst schlag' ein Hageldonnerwetter drein!
Stemmt euch hier nicht mehr zu Hauf,
oder sonst wir schlagen drauf. –

WOMEN
(looking out of windows)

What is all this brawling and strife!
It truly freezes up the blood!
My husband surely will be there!
If only father were not there!
    Listen, you below there!
    Do have a little sense!
    Are you then all alike
    So ready for a fight?
    Oh, alas what a sight!
    Ah! God! What's become of my Hans?
    Ah! Look what a sight!
    Have you then all gone mad?
    Are your heads
    All full of wine?
    Oh murder! Murder!
    There, my man's in the fight!
    There's father! There's father!
    Look! What a sight!
    Christian! Peter!

Was ist denn da für Streit und Zank?
's wird einem wahrlich Angst und bang!
Da ist mein Mann gewiss dabei:
gewiss kommt's noch zur Schlägerei!
    He da! Ihr dort unten,
    so seid doch nur gescheit!
    Seid ihr zu Streit und Raufen
    gleich Alle so bereit?
    Was für ein Zanken und Toben!
    Da werden schon Arme erhoben!
    Hört doch! Hört doch!
    Seid ihr denn toll?
    Sind euch die Köpfe
    von Weine noch voll?
    Zu Hülfe! Zu Hülfe!
    Da schlägt sich mein Mann!
    Der Vater! der Vater!
    Sieht man das an?
    Christian! Peter!

Nicholas! Hans!	Niklaus! Hans!
Ah! How will it finish?	Auf! schreit Zeter! –
Franz, have a little sense.	Hörst du nicht, Franz?
The heads and pigtails	Gott! wie sie walken!
Waggle up and down!	's wackeln die Zöpfe!
Quick! Water here! Water here!	Wasser her! Wasser her!
Pour water on their heads below.	Giesst's ihn' auf die Köpfe!

(*The brawl is at its height with screaming and roaring.*)

MAGDALENE
(*at the window, wringing her hands in despair*)

Oh Heaven! David! Lord, what ill luck!	Ach Himmel! Meine Noth ist gross! –
Hear me now David!	David! So hör' mich doch nur an!
And let the Marker there go free!	So lass' doch nur den Herren los!

POGNER
(*appears at the window in his nightgown and pulls Magdalene inside*)

How now! Eva! Come in!	Um Gott! Eva! schliess' zu! –
I'll see below if all is safe!	Ich seh', ob im Haus unten Ruh'!

(*He shuts the window and appears below at the door. Sachs has put out his light and set the door ajar, so as to watch what is happening under the lime-tree. Walther and Eva observe the riot with increasing anxiety. Walther takes her in his arms.*)

WALTHER

Now comes the time,	Jetzt gilt's zu wagen,
Let us fight our way through!	sich durchzuschlagen!

(*With drawn sword he pushes his way to the middle of the stage. Instantly Sachs rushes from his door and seizes him by the arm. At that precise moment another of the Nightwatchman's horn-calls is heard and the women pour water onto the riot. The men run off in every direction, doors close, and even the neighbours shut their windows, so that very quickly the stage is empty.*) [25]

POGNER
(*on the steps*)

Ho! Lene! Where are you?	[22a]He! Lene! Wo bist du?

SACHS
(*pushing Eva, almost fainting, up the steps*)

Go in, Mistress Lene!	In's Haus, Jungfer Lene!

(*Pogner hustles Eva into the house. Sachs gives David a blow with his strap and kicks him into the shop – he drags Walther in as well, barring the door behind him. Beckmesser, much battered, escapes through the crowd. Once the street and alley are empty and the windows closed, the nightwatchman enters, rubs his eyes and looks around in surprise; shaking his head he sings his verse with a tremulous voice.*)

NIGHTWATCHMAN

Hark to what I say good people,	Hört ihr Leut', und lasst euch sagen:
Eleven strikes in the steeple;	die Glock' hat Eilfe geschlagen,
Defend yourselves from spectre and sprite,	Bewahrt euch vor Gespenstern und Spuck,
That no power of ill your souls affright!	dass kein böser Geist eur' Seel' beruck'!
Praise ye God the Lord!	Lobet Gott den Herrn!

[25, 30]

(*A full moon shines brightly down the alley by which the nightwatchman leaves. As he turns the corner, the curtain falls quickly on the last chord.*)

Act Three

Scene One. *In Sach's workshop. At the back, a half-open door leads to the street. The door of the inner room is on the right. On the left, is a window looking into the alley with flowers in pots in front and a work bench beside it. Sachs sits at this window in a great arm-chair, the bright morning sun streaming in on him; he has a large folio on his lap and is absorbed in reading. David peeps round the street door; seeing that Sachs does not notice him, he enters with a basket on his arm, and quickly hides it under the other work bench; when he is sure that Sachs does not notice him, he takes it out and investigates the contents. He is about to eat them when Sachs, still unconscious of his presence, turns over a leaf of his book with a loud rustle.* [32, 33]

DAVID
(starts, hides the food and turns around)

Here Master! Here!	Gleich! Meister! Hier! –
The shoes were taken early	Die Schuh' sind abgegeben
To Master Beckmesser's house,	in Herrn Beckmesser's Quartier. –
I thought just now you were calling?	Mir war's, ihr rief't mich eben?

(aside)

He acts as if I were not here.	Er thut, als säh' er mich nicht?
He must be cross, or he would speak.	Da ist er bös', wenn er nicht spricht!

(He approaches Sachs humbly.)

Oh Master won't you forgive?	Ach, Meister! wollt ihr mir verzeih'n!
Did a perfect prentice yet live?	Kann ein Lehrbub' vollkommen sein?
If you knew my Lene as I,	Kenntet ihr die Lene, wie ich,
Your forgiveness you'd not deny.	dann vergäb't ihr mir sicherlich.
She is so good, so sweet to me,	Sie ist so gut, so sanft für mich,
And looks at me oft so tenderly.	und blickt mich oft an, so innerlich:
When you are harsh, then she is kind;	wenn ihr mich schlagt, streichelt sie mich,
Her smiles will drive all cares from my mind;	und lächelt dabei holdseliglich,
When I am hungry she brings me food,	muss ich cariren, füttert sie mich,
And she is always so sweet and good!	und ist in Allem gar liebelich.
But last night when she heard of Sir Walther	Nur gestern, weil der Junker versungen,
She took away the basket I longed for.	hab' ich den Korb ihr nicht abgerungen:
That made me sad; and when I found	das schmerzte mich; und da ich fand,
That evening a man outside her house	dass Nachts Einer vor dem Fenster stand,
Who sang to her and howled like mad,	und sang zu ihr, und schrie wie toll,
I fell upon him tooth and nail.	da hieb ich dem den Buckel voll.
Why make so great a matter of that?	Wie käm' nun da 'was Gross' drauf an?
Besides, for our love, it has turned out well!	Auch hat's unsrer Lieb' gar gut gethan;
And Lene has explained the matter to me,	die Lene hat eben mir Alles erklärt,
And today ribbons and flowers sent to me.	und zum Fest Blumen und Bänder bescheert.

(increasingly worried, he breaks out)

Ah Master! Speak one word I pray!	Ach, Meister! sprecht doch nur ein Wort!

(aside)

If I'd only thought to take the food away!	Hätt' ich nur die Wurst und den Kuchen fort! –

SACHS
(has read on undisturbed. He closes the book. Startled by the noise, David stumbles and falls unintentionally on his knees before him. Sachs looks away over his book, and over David's head, staring at the table at the back. David looks up at him, frightened.) [9]

Flowers and ribbons do I see?	Blumen und Bänder seh' ich dort: –
They look so fresh and so fair.	schaut hold und jugendlich aus!
How do they come to be there?	Wie kamen die mir in's Haus?

DAVID
(surprised at Sachs's friendliness)

Ah Master! Today's a festive day,	Ei, Meister: 's ist heut' hoch festlicher Tag;
When each one dresses the best he may.	da putzt sich jeder, so schön er mag.

SACHS
(still softly, as if to himself)

Is it a wedding day?   Wär Hochzeitsfest?

DAVID

         Ah, so it could be,   Ja, käm's so weit,
If Lene would marry me!   dass David erst die Lene freit!

SACHS

Your bachelor party was last night?   's war Polterabend, dünkt mich doch?

DAVID
(aside)

Bachelor evening? Now trouble's in sight!   Polterabend? – Da krieg' ich's wohl noch? –
                 (aloud)
Forgive it Master, forget I pray!   Verzeiht das, Meister! Ich bitt', vergesst!
Today is St John's Midsummer day.   Wir feiern ja heut' Johannisfest.

SACHS

Midsummer day?   Johannisfest?

DAVID
(aside)

         Deaf he must be!   Hört er heut' schwer?

SACHS

You know your verses? Then sing to me!   Kannst du dein Sprüchlein? Sag' es her!

DAVID
(who has gradually got up)

My verses? Yes, you will see!   Mein Sprüchlein? Denk', ich kann es gut.
                 (aside)
'Tis well! The Master is pleased with me.   'Setzt nichts! der Meister ist wohlgemuth!
                 (aloud)
"St John baptized in Jordan's tide" –   [30] "Am Jordan Sankt Johannes stand" –

(in his agitation he sings his lines to the melody of Beckmesser's serenade; he is stopped by Sachs's gesture of astonishment)

SACHS

What's that?   Wa-was?

DAVID

Forgive me again!   Verzeiht das Gewirr:
I sang you the bachelor evening's tune.   mich machte der Polterabend.
         (He collects himself and stands up properly.)
"St John baptized in Jordan's stream   [13] "Am Jordan Sankt Johannes stand,
   All folk of every nation;   all Volk der Welt zu taufen:
From Nuremberg a woman came   ham aus ein Weib aus fernem Land
   To seek from him salvation: aus Nürnberg gar gelaufen;
Her little child was by her side,   sein Söhnlein trug's zum Uferrand,
   And took both name and blessing.   empfing da Tauf' und Namen;
Then glowing with maternal pride,   doch als sie dann sich heimgewandt,
   To Nuremberg returning,   nach Nürnberg wieder kamen,
She soon found in her native land,   in deutschen Land gar bald sich fand's,
That he who took by Jordan's strand   dass wer am Ufer des Jordans
   Johannes for his name,   Johannes war genannt,
   On the Pegnitz changed to Hans."   an der Pegnitz hiess der Hans."
                 (warmly)
Ah, Master! It is your Saint's day too!   Herr Meister! 's ist heut' eu'r Namenstag!
How could I be so forgetful now!   Nein! Wie man so 'was vergessen mag! –
Here! Take these flowers! They are yours,   Hier! hier, die Blümen sind für euch,
The ribbons, and now what else have I got?   die Bänder, – und was nur Alles noch gleich?
Oh yes, look! Master, look at this pastry!   Ja hier! schaut, Meister! Herrlicher Kuchen!
And here's a sausage, oh won't you taste it?   Möchtet ihr nicht auch die Wurst
                           versuchen?

SACHS
(still quietly, without moving)

Best thanks my boy! Keep them yourself,	Schön Dank, mein Jung'! behalt's für dich!
To festival meadow with me shall you go.	Doch heut' auf die Wiese begleitest du mich:
With ribbons and flowers and fine array	mit Blumen und Bändern putz' dich fein;
You shall go as my Page today!	[3] sollst mein stattlicher Herold sein!

DAVID

Might I not be your best man instead?	Sollt' ich nicht lieber Brautführer sein? –
Master, ah Master, once more you must wed.	Meister! lieb' Meister! ihr müsst wieder frei'n!

SACHS

Would you like then a Mistress here?	Hätt'st wohl gern eine Meist'rin im Haus?

DAVID

The house would look so much finer I'm sure.	Ich mein', es säh' doch viel stattlicher aus.

SACHS

Who knows? But time may tell.	Wer weiss! Kommt Zeit, kommt Rath.

DAVID

Time's here!	's ist Zeit!

SACHS

Then may the answer soon appear.	Da wär' der Rath wohl nicht weit?

DAVID

Of course! Everybody says the same thing,	Gewiss geh'n Reden schon hin und wieder.
That Beckmesser will have no chance if you sing!	Den Beckmesser, denk' ich, säng't ihr doch nieder?
I think that today he will not succeed.	Ich mein', dass der heut' sich nicht wichtig macht.

SACHS

Quite likely, that was also my thought.	Wohl möglich! Hab mir's auch schon bedacht. –
Now go; disturb not Sir Walther's rest.	Jetzt geh'; doch stör' mir den Junker nicht!
Come back again when you are dressed.	Komm wieder, wenn du schön gericht'.

DAVID
(Moved, he kisses Sachs's hand, collects his things and goes into the next room.)

He was never like this, though sometimes kind!	So war er noch nie, wenn sonst auch gut!
Now the feel of his leather strap has gone from my mind!	Kann mir gar nicht mehr denken, wie der Knieriemen thut!

SACHS
(Still with the folio on his lap, he leans his arms upon it; his talk with David does not seem to have disturbed his meditation.)

Fools! Fools!	[32] Wahn, Wahn!
Everywhere fools!	Ueberall Wahn!
All vainly do I look	Wohin ich forschend blick'
And seek in ancient book,	in Stadt- und Welt-Chronik,
The cause of these delusions	den Grund mir aufzufinden,
That drive men on to fight,	warum gar bis auf's Blut
And fill their minds with confusion	die Leut sich quälen und schinden
And aimless crazy spite!	in unnütz toller Wuth!
For only grief	Hat Keiner Lohn
Is their reward,	noch Dank davon:
They fly the foe	in Flucht geschlagen
Yet think they pursue him;	wähnt er zu jagen
Hear not their own	Hört nicht sein eigen
Wild cry of pain,	Schmerz-Gekreisch,
When their own flesh they tear and maim	wenn er sich wühlt in's eig'ne Fleisch,

And glory in their anguish!	wähnt Lust sich zu erzeigen.
For this how find a name?	Wer giebt den Namen an?
The folly's still the same,	's bleibt halt der alte Wahn,
It haunts our footsteps ever,	ohn' den nichts mag geschehen,
And spoils our best endeavour!	's mag gehen oder stehen!
Stayed in its course,	steht's wo im Lauf,
It sleeps but greater strength to gain:	er schläft nur neue Kraft sich an;
Soon it awakes	gleich wacht er auf,
And lo! Who can restrain it then?	dann schaut wer ihn bemeistern kann! –
In peaceful ways well grounded,	Wie friedsam treuer Sitten,
Content in fruitful work,	getrost in That und Werk,
By friendly folk surrounded	liegt nicht in Deutschland's Mitten
My cherished Nüremberg! [23, 34]	mein liebes Nürenberg!
But on an evening late,	Doch eines Abends spat,
A maiden and her lover	ein Unglück zu verhüten
Their youthful passion discover,	bei jungendheissen Gemüthen,
And then, careless of fate,	ein Mann weiss sich nicht Rath;
A shoemaker interfering	ein Schuster in seinem Laden
Sets the old folly stirring:	zieht an des Wahnes Faden;
Then soon his neighbours awaken,	wie bald auf Gassen und Strassen
By rage and anger shaken!	fängt der da an zu rasen;
Man, wife and youth and child,	Mann, Weib, Gesell und Kind,
Rush to the fray as though gone wild;	fällt sich an wie toll und blind;
And Folly brings the blessing	und will's der Wahn geseg'nen,
Of strife and blows unceasing,	nun muss es Prügel regnen,
Each fellow must belabour [31]	mit Hieben, Stoss' und Dreschen
With furious rage his neighbour.	den Wuthesbrand zu löschen. –
God knows how that befel!	Gott weiss, wie das geschah? –
Some pixie wove the spell.	Ein Kobold half wohl da!
A glow-worm sought his mate in vain; [25]	Ein Glühwurm fand sein Weibchen nicht;
From him it was the mischief came.	der hat den Schaden angericht'. –
The elder it was – Midsummer eve!	Der Flieder war's: – Johannisnacht. –
But now has dawned Midsummer day!	Nun aber kam Johannis-Tag: –
Now let us see what Sachs can do, [15]	jetzt schau'n wir, wie Hans Sachs es macht,
So that the folly may be turned	dass er den Wahn fein lenken mag,
And used for nobler work.	ein edler Werk zu thun;
For if it still can lurk, [23, 15, 2]	denn lässt er uns nicht ruh'n,
E'en here in Nuremberg,	selbst hier in Nürenberg,
We'll set it such a task	so sei's um solche Werk',
As seldom can succeed without it,	die selten vor gemeinen Dingen,
And needs one who is mad to start it.	und nie ohn' ein'gen Wahn gelingen.

(*Walther enters by the inner door. He pauses there a moment and looks at Sachs, who turns and lets the book slide to the floor.*)

SACHS
[21b]

My friend, good morning! Rested I hope!	Grüss Gott, mein Junker! Ruhtet ihr noch?
Your night was short, I trust you slept?	Ihr wachtet lang': nun schlieft ihr doch?

WALTHER
(*very quietly*)

A little, but my sleep was good.	Ein wenig, aber fest und gut.

SACHS

So then you rise in better mood?	So ist euch nun wohl bass zu Muth?

WALTHER
(*still very quietly*)

I had a rare and wondrous dream.	Ich hatt' ein wunderschönen Traum.

SACHS

A welcome sign: what dreamt you, pray?	Das deutet Gut's! Erzählt mir den.

WALTHER

I dare not think what it could mean	Ihn selbst zu denken wag' ich kaum;
For fear that it should fade away.	Ich fürcht' ihn mir vergeh'n zu seh'n.

SACHS

My friend, that is the poet's task	[21b] Mein Freund, das grad' ist Dichter's Werk,
Too seek in dreams what will come to pass.	dass er sein Träumen deut' und merk'.
In truth the deepest wisdom man has known	Glaubt mir, des Menschen wahrster Wahn
Has been what dreams have shown.	wird ihm in Traume aufgethan:
All verses that our poets write	all' Dichtkunst und Poeterei
Are truths that dreams have brought to light.	ist nichts als Wahrtraum-Deuterei.
Did not your dream suggest a way	Was gilt's, es gab der Traum euch ein,
To win the Master's prize today!	wie heut' ihr sollet Meister sein?

WALTHER
(very quietly)

No, from your guild and all its Masters,	Nein! von der Zunft und ihren Meistern
My dream would bring me new disasters.	wollt' sich mein Traumbild nicht begeistern.

SACHS

Yet might it teach the magic spell	Doch lehrt' es wohl den Zauberspruch,
To make you Mastersinger?	mit dem ihr sie gewännet?

WALTHER
(with greater animation)

How can you think since what befell,	Wie wännt ihr doch, nach solchem Bruch,
That any hope may linger?	wenn ihr noch Hoffnung kennet!

SACHS

Yet hope is still within me burning:	Die Hoffnung lass' ich mir nicht mindern,
It fills my heart to overflowing.	nichts stiess sie noch über'n Haufen:
Were't not so, 'stead of your flight delaying,	wär's nicht, glaubt, statt eu're Flucht zu hindern,
I myself with you, now were going!	wär' ich selbst mit euch fortgelaufen!
I beg you no more anger feel!	Drum bitt' ich, lasst den Groll jetzt ruh'n;
You have with men of honour to deal.	ihr habt's mit Ehrenmännern zu thun;
They make mistakes, all unawares,	die irren sich, und sind bequem,
And think the only right way is theirs.	dass man auf ihre Weise sie nähm'.
And surely a man who grants a prize	Wer Preise erkennt, und Preise stellt,
May ask what he finds pleasing in his eyes.	der will am End' auch, dass man ihm gefällt.
Your song has filled them with dark dismay;	Eu'r Lied das hat ihnen bang' gemacht;
And with good cause, for, truth to say,	und das mit Recht: denn wohl bedacht,
A song so full of poet's passion	mit solchem Dicht – und Liebesfeuer
May kindle our daughters in wicked fashion.	verführt man wohl Töchter zum Abenteuer;
But to praise long-lasting married bliss,	doch für liebseligen Ehestand
We've other words and tunes than this.	man andre Wort' und Weisen fand.

WALTHER
(smiling)

I know what you mean; I've heard them too;	Die kenn' ich nun auch, seit dieser Nacht:
For only last night they rang through the street.	es hat viel Lärm auf der Gasse gemacht.

SACHS
(laughing)

Yes, yes! That's true! My beating time	Ja, ja! Schon gut! Den Takt dazu
You heard that too! But let that go	den hörtet ihr auch! – Doch, lasst dem Ruh';
And hark to my counsel, short and good:	und folgt meinem Rathe, kurz und gut,
Fashion to a Mastersong your mood!	fasst zu einem Meisterliede Muth.

WALTHER

A beauteous song, a Mastersong:	Ein schönes Lied, ein Meisterlied:
I've always thought that they were one.	wie fass' ich da den Unterschied?

SACHS
(softly)

My friend, in joyful days of youth	[27] Mein Freund! in holder Jugendzeit,
When first our souls are captured	wenn uns von mächt'gen Trieben

In joy of love enraptured,
When hearts are beating proud and high,
The gift of song is given
To all by kindly Heaven:
'Tis spring that sings, not we.
Through summer, fall and winter's chill
When cares of life are pressing,
Though marriage brings its blessing,
Children and business, strife, ill-will,
Only those who still have kept then
This gift of song from Heaven, [6a]
Then Masters they will be!

zum sel'gen ersten Lieben
die Brust sich schwellet hoch und weit,
ein schönes Lied zu singen
mocht' vielen da gelingen:
der Lenz, der sang für sie.
Kam Sommer, Herbst und Winterszeit,
viel Noth und Sorg' im Leben,
manch' ehlich Glück daneben,
Kindtauf, Geschäfte, Zwist und Streit:
denen's dann noch will gelingen
ein schönes Lied zu singen,
seht, Meister nennt man die. –

WALTHER
(tenderly and fervently)

I love a maid and long to prove,
In lasting wedlock, all my love.

Ich lieb' ein Weib und will es frei'n,
mein dauernd Ehgemahl zu sein.

SACHS

Then let the Master-rules now speed you,
That they may truly guide and lead you,
And help to keep untainted
What spring and youth have planted
Amidst youth's pleasure
So the treasure
Deep in the heart in secret laid,
Through power of song shall never fade!

Die Meisterregeln lernt bei Zeiten,
dass sie getreulich euch geleiten,
und helfen wohl bewahren,
was in der Jungend Jahren
in holden Triebe
Lenz und Liebe
euch unbewusst in's Herz gelegt,
das ihr das unverloren hegt.

WALTHER

Tell me, then, if so high they stand,
By whom of old the rules were planned.

Steh'n sie nun in so hohem Ruf,
wer ist es, der die Regeln schuf?

SACHS

By Masters worn with pain of living:
With world's distress and anguish striving:
By heavy cares o'erweighted,
A vision they created,
Thus to recapture
Their youthful rapture
And keep the memory fresh and true
Of all the springs that once they knew.

Das waren hoch-bedürft'ge Meister,
von Lebensmüh' bedrängte Geister;
in ihrer Nöthen Wildniss
sie schufen sich ein Bildniss,
dass ihnen bliebe
der Jungendliebe
ein Angedenken klar und fest,
dran sich der Lenz erkennen lässt.

WALTHER

But when their spring had long been over,
What then could they in dreams recover?

Doch, wem der Lenz schon lang entronnen,
wie wird er aus dem Bild gewonnen?

SACHS

Well then they do as best they can:
So let me, as a humble man,
Teach you our rules of singing,
In them you may find new [21a, b]
meaning. –
Pen, ink and paper ready you see:
I'll write the words you sing to me!

Er frischt es an, so gut er kann:
drum möcht' ich, als bedürft'ger Mann,
will ich euch die Regeln lehren,
Solt ihr sie mir neu erklären,
Seht, hier ist Tinte, Feder, Papier:
ich schreib's euch auf, dictirt ihr mir!

WALTHER

I know not how I can begin.

Wie ich's begänne, wüsst' ich kaum.

SACHS

Think only of your morning dream!

Erzählt mir euren Morgentraum!

WALTHER

Through all the rules that you have taught,
It seems my dream has come to nought.

Durch eurer Regeln gute Lehr',
ist mir's, als ob verwischt er wär'!

SACHS

Then you the poet's art must try;
Dreams that are lost can be found thereby.

Grad' nehmt die Dichtkunst jetzt zue Hand;
mancher durch sie das Verlor'ne fand.

WALTHER

Was it no dream, but only art?	Dann wär's nicht Traum, doch Dichterei?

SACHS

The two are friends, not far apart.	Sind Freunde beid', steh'n gern sich bei.

WALTHER

But how should I by Rule begin?	Wie fang' ich nach der Regel an?

SACHS

First make your rules, then follow them.	Ihr stellt sie selbst, und folgt ihr dann:
Think only of your dream of beauty:	Gedenkt des schönen Traum's am Morgen:
All else shall be Hans Sachs's duty.	für's And're lasst Hans Sachs nur sorgen!

WALTHER

(standing by the work bench as Sachs writes down his poem)

[2]

"Warm in the sunlight at dawning of day, [7]	"Morgenlich leuchtend in rosigem Schein,
When blossoms rare	von Blüth' und Duft
Made sweet the air,	geschwellt die Luft,
With beauty glowing	voll aller Wonnen
Past all knowing,	nie ersonnen,
A garden round me lay,	ein Garten lud mich ein
Cheering my way."	Gast ihm zu sein."

(He pauses.)

SACHS

That was a "Strophe", now heed my word,	Das war ein Stollen: nun achtet wohl,
That one just like it must now be heard.	dass ganz ein gleicher ihm folgen soll.

WALTHER

But why just like?	Warum ganz gleich?

SACHS

That men may know,	Damit man seh',
A wife like yourself you've chosen so.	ihr wähltet euch gleich ein Weib zur Eh'.

WALTHER
(continuing)

"High o'er the garden a tree did arise:	"Wonnig entragend dem seligen Raum
The golden store,	bot gold'ner Frucht
Its branches bore,	heilsaft'ge Wucht
So richly thronging,	mit holdem Prangen
Stirred my longing,	dem Verlangen
When in the verdant shade	an duft'ger Zweige Saum
I saw my prize."	herrlich ein Baum."

(He pauses.)

SACHS

You ended in another key:	Ihr schlosset nicht im gleichen Ton:
That Masters blame you know;	das macht den Meistern Pein;
But I, Hans Sachs, your meaning see;	Doch nimmt Hans Sachs die Lehr' davon,
In springtime it must be so.	im Lenz wohl müss' es so sein. –
Now sing to me an "After song".	Nun stellt mir einen Abgesang.

WALTHER

What does that mean?	Was soll nun der?

SACHS

If rightly sung	Ob euch gelang
It shows that by your mating,	ein rechtes Paar zu finden,
The child of your creating,	das zeigt sich jetzt an den Kinden.
Is like the parents, yet not the same,	Den Stollen ähnlich, doch nicht gleich,
And has its rhyme and tone and name;	an eig'nen Reim und Tönen reich;
And when a child can show such art	dass man es recht schlank und selbstig find',
It surely warms the parent's heart:	das freut die Aeltern an dem Kind:
Thus to your Strophes give an end	und euren Stollen giebt's den Schluss,
That all things together may blend.	dass nichts davon abfallen muss.

WALTHER
(continuing)

"How shall I name
The radiant wonder there revealed?
A maiden fair stood by me there,
Her grace no mortal e'er beheld:
    Then like a bride
    She folded me soft on her breast;
    Her eyes were gazing
    Her hand upraising,
Where shone the fruit's golden hue,
She showed the place where grew
    The laurel tree."

"Sei euch vertraut
welch' hehres Wunder mir gesch'n:
an meiner Seite stand ein Weib,
so hold und schön ich nie geseh'n;
    gleich einer Braut
    unfasste sie sanft meinen Leib;
    mit Augen winkend,
    die Hand wies blinkend,
was ich verlangend begehrt,
die Frucht so hold und werth
    vom Lebensbaum."

SACHS
(concealing his emotion) [32]

In troth I call that an Aftersong!
See how the verse now flows along!
    But with the melody
    You were a trifle free.
Now I don't say that seems a fault to me:
Just that at first, it's perplexing.
And to old men that is vexing.
A second verse must you now compose,
To fix in mind how the first one goes.
But still I'm not sure, so good does it seem,

How much is poem, and how much dream.

Das nenn' ich mir ein Abgesang:
seht, wie der ganze Bar gelang
    nur mit der Melodei
    seid ihr ein wenig frei;
doch sag' ich nicht, dass es ein Fehler sei;
nur ist's nicht leicht zu behalten,
und das ärgert unsre Alten! –
Jetzt richtet mir noch einen zweiten Bar,
damit man merk' welch' der erste war.
Auch weiss ich noch nicht, so gut ihr's
    gereimt,
was ihr gedichtet, was ihr geträumt.

WALTHER

"Sunset was glowing with heavenly light,
    O'er dying day
    While there I lay;
    My heart on fire
    With one desire,
From eyes so wondrous bright,
    To drink delight.
Night closes round me to darken the place!

    Afar, yet near,
    Two stars appear,
    In day's declining
    Softly shining,
Their balm of heavenly grace
    Falls on my face.
    There, on a height,
A crystal fountain at my feet,
From earth outpours its limpid stream,
    With swelling tone, so full and sweet.
    Sparkling and bright,
New gathering stars on me gleam as,
    Gaily dancing,
    Through branches glancing,
Their golden lustre they shed;
Not fruit but stars o'erspread
    The laurel tree."

"Abendlich glühend in himmlischer Pracht
    verschied der Tag,
    wie dort ich lag;
    aus ihren Augen
    Wonne saugen,
Verlangen einz'ger Macht
    in mir nur wacht'. –
Nächtlich umdämmert der Blick sich mir
    bricht!
    wie weit so nah
    beschienen da
    zwei lichte Sterne
    aus der Ferne
durch schlanker Zweige Licht
    hehr mein Gesicht. –
    Lieblich ein Quell
auf stiller Höhe dort mir rauscht;
jetzt schwellt er an sein hold Getön'
    so süss und stark ich's nie erlauscht:
    leuchtend und hell
wie strahlten die Sterne da schön;
    zu Tanz und Reigen
    in Laub und Zweigen
der gold'nen sammeln sich mehr,
statt Frucht ein Sternenheer
    im Lorbeerbaum." –

SACHS
(deeply moved, softly)

Friend, your dream told you the truth
And bravely you sing the second verse.
Make a third one now to show more clearly
Your vision's meaning in all its glory.

Freund! eu'r Traumbild wies euch wahr:
gelungen ist auch der zweite Bar.
Wolltet ihr noch einen dritten dichten,
des Traumes Deutung würd' er berichten.

WALTHER
(rising quickly)

How can I now? Enough of words!

Wie fänd' ich die? Genug der Wort'!

105

SACHS

(rising at the same time and approaching Walther with friendly decision)

Then deed and rhyme at proper time!	[21b]Dann Wort und That am rechten Ort! –
I beg you well the tune remember,	Drum bitt' ich, merkt mir gut die Weise;
Right well it goes with such a theme,	gar lieblich drin sich's dichten lässt:
And, when before the folk you sing it,	[23] und singt ihr sie im weit'ren Kreise,
Hold fast in your mind that morning dream.	dann haltet mir auch das Traumbild fest.

WALTHER

What is your plan?	Was habt ihr vor?

SACHS

Your trusty squire,	Eu'r treuer Knecht
Followed you here with your attire;	fand sich mit Sack' und Tasch' zurecht;
The clothes that for the wedding feast	die Kleider, drin am Hochzeitsfest
At home you would be wearing,	daheim bei euch ihr wolltet prangen,
Your squire has now come hither bearing!	die liess er her zu mir gelangen; –
An angel must have shown the nest	ein Täubchen zeigt' ihm wohl das Nest,
In which his master dreamed.	darin sein Junker träumt':
So to your room now follow me.	drum folgt mir jetzt in's Kämmerlein!
With garments richly trimmed	Mit Kleiden, wohlgesäumt,
Should we both today apparelled be;	sollen Beide wir gezieret sein,
Since Fate has called to daring deed.	wann's Stattliches zu wagen gilt: –
Now come, if we are both agreed.	drum kommt, seid ihr gleich mir gewillt!

(Walther grasps Sachs's hand. Sachs leads him to the inner door, opens it and follows him out.)
[16a, 23, 21a, 30, 32, 22a]

Scene Three. *Beckmesser appears outside the shop window, looking in, in great perturbation. Finding the shop empty he enters hastily. He is dressed very richly, but seems very miserable. He peeps again carefully round the shop from the doorway. He then limps forwards, winces in pain and rubs his back. After a few more steps forwards his knees give way. He rubs them. He sits on the cobbler's stool, but starts up again in pain. He contemplates the stool and his thoughts seem to become more and more agitated. He is distressed by the most agonising memories and fancies; getting ever more uneasy, he begins to wipe perspiration from his brow. He limps round more and more restlessly, looking around him. As if pursued from all sides, he stumbles here and there and tries to save himself from falling; he totters to the table, holds onto it, and stares before him. Weak and in despair, he looks around. At length he notices Pogner's house through the window, and he limps towards it with difficulty; looking at the window opposite he tries to assume a bold manner as he thinks of Walther. Then angry thoughts arise which he tries to fight down. Jealousy overcomes him. He strikes his forehead. He fancies that he hears again the mocking of the women and boys in the alley; he turns away in a rage and slams the window shut. Much upset he turns again to the work-table; he contemplates it while he seems to be thinking up a new tune. He notices the paper with Sachs's handwriting; he picks it up curiously; examines it with growing excitement and finally breaks out in fury.* [7]

BECKMESSER

A trial song! By Sachs! Is it true?	Ein Werbelied! Von Sachs? – ist's wahr?
Ha! Now all is clear to me!	Ah! Nun wird mir alles klar!

(He hears the inner door open, starts and hurriedly puts the paper in his pocket. Sachs, dressed for the festival, comes forward and stops when he sees Beckmesser.)

SACHS

What you, Sir Marker! Here so early?	[22a]Sieh da! Herr Schreiber? Auch am Morgen?
Your shoes do not still give trouble surely?	Euch machen die Schuh' doch nicht mehr Sorgen?

BECKMESSER

The devil! So thin, worse than you've made before;	Den Teufel! So dünn war ich noch nie beschuht:
Through them I feel the smallest stone!	Fühl' durch die Sohle den feinsten Kies!

SACHS

On Marker's art blame that alone;	Mein Merkersprüchlein wirkte dies:
Marking your faults has made them so thin.	trieb sie mit Merkerzeichen so weich.

BECKMESSER

Now no more tricks! Though your wit is keen,
I know, friend Sachs, just what you mean.

Your trick of yesterday
You will not soon forget.
So that I should not obstruct your way,
You'd raise the neighbours and make 'em fight.

Schon gut der Witz'! Und genug der Streich'!
Glaubt mir, Freund Sachs, jetzt kenn' ich euch!

der Spass von dieser Nacht,
der wird euch noch gedacht:
dass ich euch nur nicht im Wege sei,
schuft ihr gar Aufruhr und Meuterei!

SACHS

'Twas bachelor party, let me remind you;
And the folk today a bride may assign you:
The madder the fun, you see,
The better your luck will be!

's war Polterabend, lasst euch bedeuten:
eure Hochzeit spuckte unter den Leuten;
je toller es da hergeh',
je besser bekommt's der Eh'.

BECKMESSER
(furiously)

Oh, cobbler full of cunning,
I see such trouble coming!
You always were my foe,
And now your craft I know.
The maid for whom I've waited,
For me alone created;
All widowers to shame,
On her you fix your aim!
'Tis Master Sachs's pleasure,
To win the goldsmith's treasure,
And so before the Guild,
Our ears with stuff he filled;
A maiden's fancy fooling,
That she might heed his schooling,
And, to the shame of all,
Her choice on him might fall.
    And so! And so!
    Ah now I know!
With voice and hammer ringing,
You sought to drown my singing,
Lest she should understand,
Another stood there at hand.
    Ha, ha! Ho, ho!
    'Tis even so?
Directed by your cunning,
The boys in packs came running,
With cudgels for the fray,
To drive me from your way!
    Ow, ow! Ow, ow!
    I'm black and blue,
And shamed before the maiden too!
With tooth and nail they tore me:
Ne'er a tailor could restore me!
Suspicions fill me,
    They meant to kill me!
Yet by luck I got away,
That I my debt might pay.
Go forth when all assemble,
Today your voice may tremble.
    Though I've been thrashed
    Don't laugh too soon,
For I can still put you out of tune.

O Schuster, voll von Ränken
und pöbelhaften Schwänken,
du warst mein Feind von je:
nun hör' ob hell ich seh'!
Die ich mir auserkoren,
die ganz für mich geboren,
zu aller Wittwer Schmach,
der Jungfer stellst du nach.
Dass sich Herr Sachs erwerbe
des Goldschmied's reiches Erbe,
im Meister-Rath zur Hand
auf Klauseln er bestand,
ein Mägdlein zu bethören,
das nur auf ihn sollt' hören,
und, And'ren abgewandt,
zu ihm allein sich fand.
    Darum! darum! –
    wär' ich so dumm? –
mit Schreien und mit Klopfen
wollt' er mein Lied zustopfen,
dass nicht dem Kind werd' kund
wie auch ein And'rer bestund!
    Ja ja! – Ha ha!
    Hab' ich dich da?
Aus seiner Schuster-Stuben
hetzt' endlich er die Buben
mit Knüppeln auf mich her,
dass meiner los er wär'!
    Au au! Au au!
    Wohl grün und blau,
zum Spott der allerliebsten Frau,
zerschlagen und zerprügelt,
dass kein Schneider mich aufbügelt!
    Gar auf mein Leben
    war's angegeben!
Doch kam ich noch so davon,
dass ich die That euch lohn'!
zieht heut' nur aus zum Singen,
merkt auf, wie's mag gelingen;
    bin ich gezwackt
    auch und zerhackt,
euch bring' ich doch sicher aus dem Takt!

SACHS

Good friend, your wits are overcast.
Think what you will of what is past:
Through all your jealousy you're blind;
For wooing never crossed my mind.

Gut Freund, ihr seid in argem Wahn!
Glaubt was ihr wollt, dass ich gethan,
gebt eure Eifersucht nur hin;
zu werben kommt mir nicht in Sinn.

That's a lie! I know you better.   Lug und Trug! Ich weiss es besser.

SACHS

What fancy is this, Master Beckmesser?   Was fällt euch nur ein, Meister Beckmesser?
What I have in mind concerns you not: Was ich sonst im Sinn, geht euch nichts an:
But trust that no wooing is in my thought.   doch glaubt, ob der Werbung seid ihr im
    Wahn.

BECKMESSER

You will not sing?   Ihr säng't heut' nicht?

SACHS

    Not as suitor.   Nicht zur Wette.

BECKMESSER

Not sing, today?   Kein Werbelied?

SACHS

    You need not fear.   Gewisslich, nein!

BECKMESSER

But what if I have a proof you mean to?   Wenn ich aber drob ein Zeugnis hätte?
(He feels in his pocket.)

SACHS
(looking at the table)

It was here, the paper, you took it then?   Das Gedicht? Hier liess ich's: – stecktet
    ihr's ein?

BECKMESSER
(producing the paper)

Is this not your hand?   Ist das eure Hand?

SACHS

    Ah, was it that?   Ja, – war es das?

BECKMESSER

The writing is fresh!   Ganz frisch noch die Schrift?

SACHS

    And the ink is still wet!   Und die Tinte noch nass!

BECKMESSER

May be, 'tis a biblical song?   's wär' wohl gar ein biblisches Lied?

SACHS

To count on that you would be wrong!   Der fehlte wohl, wer darauf rieth.

BECKMESSER

Well then?   Nun denn?

SACHS

    How now?   Wie doch?

BECKMESSER

    You ask?   Ihr fragt?

SACHS

    What more?   Was noch?

BECKMESSER

That you, with your integrity,   Dass ihr mit aller Biederkeit
The worst of rogues and tricksters I find.   der ärgste aller Spitzbuben seid!

SACHS

May be, but yet I was never known   Mag sein! Doch hab' ich noch nie entwandt,
To pocket things I did not own.   was ich auf fremden Tischen fand: –

And so that you may not be called a thief,	und dass man von euch auch nicht übles denkt,
To save you from that I give you the song.	behaltet das Blatt, es sei euch geschenkt.

[21b]

BECKMESSER
(highly elated and surprised)

Good Lord! A song! A song by Sachs?	Herr Gott! . . . Ein Gedicht! . . . Ein Gedicht von Sachs? . . .
But wait, should he try to trick me again!	Doch halt', dass kein neuer Schad' mir erwachs'!
The song you have, no doubt, memorised?	Ihr habt's wohl schon recht gut memorirt?

SACHS

You need have no fear on my account.	Seid meinethalb doch nur unbeirrt!

BECKMESSER

You give me the song?	Ihr lasst mir das Blatt?

SACHS

Your conscience to clear.	Damit ihr kein Dieb.

BECKMESSER

To use as I like?	Und mach' ich Gebrauch?

SACHS

That's your affair.	Wie's euch belieb'.

BECKMESSER

The song I may sing?	Doch, sing' ich das Lied?

SACHS

Yes, if you dare!	Wenn's nicht zu schwer!

BECKMESSER

And if I succeed?	Und wenn ich gefiel'?

SACHS

I'll be surprised, I swear.	Das wunderte mich sehr!

BECKMESSER
(with complete confidence)

You rate yourself really, much too poorly.	Da seid ihr nun wieder zu bescheiden:
A song by Sachs is worth something, surely.	ein Lied von Sachs, das will was bedeuten!
And see now! I'm in a mess,	Und seht, wie mir's ergeht,
As no doubt you can guess,	wie's mit mir Armen steht!
The whole day I have smarted,	Erseh' ich doch mit Schmerzen,
To think how I was displayed.	das Lied, das Nachts ich sang, –
Thanks to the row you started,	Dank euren lust'gen Scherzen! –
The maiden was surely dismayed.	es machte der Pognerin bang.
How could this poor battered lover	Wie schaff' ich mir nun zur Stelle
Find time to write a song?	ein neues Lied herzu?
I'm burning and aching all over,	Ich armer, zerschlag'ner Geselle,
And it would take me too long.	wie fänd' ich heut' dazu Ruh'?
Wedlock and wooing tender,	Werbung und ehlich Leben,
For these I truly pray,	ob das mir Gott beschied,
Yet must all hope surrender,	muss ich nur grad' aufgeben,
If I've no song today.	hab' ich kein neues Lied.
A song by Sachs! Ah, surely I know,	Ein Lied von euch, dess bin ich gewiss,
With that, each hindrance will quickly go.	mit dem besieg' ich jed' Hinderniss!
Let this gift make our peace, then,	Soll ich das heute haben,
And happily cease, then,	vergessen und begraben
Our quarrels and strife,	sei Zwist, Hader und Streit,
That made us foes for life!	und was uns je entzweit.

(Looking at the paper, he frowns suddenly.)

And yet, if this were another trap?	Und doch! Wenn's nur eine Falle wär'! –
But yesterday you were my foe.	Noch gestern war't ihr mein Feind:
How is it, after all that has passed,	wie käms, dass nach so grosser Beschwer'
I find in you such a friend?	ihr's freundlich heut' mit mir meint'?

SACHS

I sat up late your shoes to make.	Ich machte euch Schuh' in später Nacht:
Who would do that for a foeman's sake?	hat man so je einen Feind bedacht?

BECKMESSER

Ah, yes! 'Tis true! Yet you must swear,	[21b]Ja ja! recht gut! – doch Eines schwört:
That whenever this song is heard	wo und wie ihr das Lied auch hört,
You never will say it is yours,	dass nie ihr euch beikommen lass't,
And, though I should win, you will make	zu sagen, das Lied sei von euch verfasst.
no claim.	

SACHS

I swear it and give my word,	Das schwör' ich und gelob' euch hier,
No claim to that song from me will be heard.	nie mich zu rühmen, das Lied sei von mir.

BECKMESSER
(rubbing his hands with delight)

Could I want more? My troubles are over:	Was will ich mehr, ich bin geborgen!
Beckmesser now will henceforth live in	Jetzt braucht sich Beckmesser nicht mehr
clover.	zu sorgen!

SACHS

My friend, I've no wish to alarm you,	Doch, Freund, ich führ's euch zu Gemüthe,
But quite sincerely now I warn you:	und rathe euch in aller Güte:
Study it long and hard,	studirt mir recht das Lied!
Not easy is the song.	Sein Vortrag ist nicht leicht:
Be sure you choose the right mode,	ob euch die Weise gerieth',
Take care the tune's not wrong.	und ihr den Ton erreicht!

BECKMESSER

Friend Sachs, as poet, you have first place,	Freund Sachs, ihr seid ein guter Poet;
But when "tones" and "modes" are in hand,	doch was Ton und Weise betrifft, gesteht,
confess,	
That I need have no fear.	da thut's mir Keiner vor!
Then open well your ear,	Drum spitzt nur fein das Ohr,
And: "Beckmesser!	Und: Beckmesser,
No-one better!"	Keiner besser!
And all your doubt will cease,	Darauf macht euch gefasst,
If you'll just let me sing in peace. [35]	wenn ihr ruhig mich singen lasst. –
But now I must learn it	Doch nun memoriren,
Well by heart:	schnell nach Haus!
That no time may be wasted,	Ohne Zeit verlieren
I must depart.	richt' ich das aus. –
Hans Sachs, my dear friend,	Hans Sachs, mein Theurer!
Your heart I misread;	ich hab' euch verkannt;
By the knight of Stolzing	durch den Abenteurer
I was misled:	war ich verrannt:
We well can spare such as he!	so einer fehlte uns blos!
We Masters from him now are free.	Den wurden wir Meister doch los! –
But all my senses	Doch mein Besinnen
Scatter and leave me!	läuft mir von hinnen:
Are my wits dazed	bin ich vewirrt,
And all astray?	und ganz verirrt?
The stanzas, the accents,	Die Sylben, die Reime,
The measure, the verses!	Die Worte, die Verse:
I stay here and chatter,	ich kleb' wie an Leime,
With feet all on fire.	und brennt doch die Ferse.
Farewell! I must go:	Ade! Ich muss fort!
We meet again.	An andrem Ort
Thanks in sincerity	dank' ich euch inniglich,
For all your friendliness;	weil ihr so minniglich;
Your word is my command,	für euch nun stimme ich,
All of your works I'll buy,	kauf' eure Werke gleich,
You shall our Marker be,	mache zum Merker euch:
But only chalk we use;	doch fein mit Kreide weich,
Mark not with hammer blows!	nicht mit dem Hammerstreich!

Marker! Marker! Marker Hans Sachs!	Merker! Merker! Merker Hans Sachs!
That Nuremberg may ever bloom and wax!	dass Nürnberg schusterlich blüh' und wachs'!

(Beckmesser, dancing about, takes leave of Sachs and hurriedly limps to the door; suddenly he returns thinking he has forgotten to pocket the song, and anxiously looks for it on the table, until he discovers it in his hand; delighted, he again gratefully embraces Sachs, and then rushes out, stumbling noisily.)

SACHS
(following Beckmesser with his eyes, thoughtfully smiling)

The man's malice will not last for long; [22a]	So ganz boshaft doch keinen ich fand,
It cannot endure day and night.	er hält's auf die Länge nicht aus!
Though we may often do what is wrong,	vergeudet mancher oft viel Verstand,
We still can tell what is right.	doch hält er auch damit Haus:
The hour of weakness comes for each one,	die schwache Stunde kommt für Jeden;
Then is the time when he will see reason.	da wird er dumm, und lässt mit sich reden. –
That Herr Beckmesser stole the song, [23]	Dass hier Herr Beckmesser ward zum Dieb,
Will help my little scheme along.	ist mir für meinen Plan sehr lieb. –

(Eva approaches the shop door from the street. He turns and sees her.)

Here's Eva! I had wondered where she was!	Sieh, Evchen! Dacht' ich doch wo sie blieb'!

Scene Four. *Eva, richly dressed in dazzling white, but rather sad and pale, comes slowly forward.* [24]

SACHS

Good day, my Eva! Why, how splendid you look,	Grüss'Gott, mein Ev'chen! Ei, wie herrlich,
How sweet and fine!	wie stolz du's heute meinst!
The hearts of old and young surrender,	Du machst wohl Jung und Alt begehrlich,
When you so brilliantly shine.	wenn du so schön erscheinst.

EVA

Master, you flatter me too much;	Meister! 's ist nicht so gefährlich:
And though my dress may be right,	und ist's dem Schneider geglückt,
You can't know what pain I'm enduring,	wer sieht dann an wo's mir beschwerlich,
Because my shoe is tight!	wo still der Schuh mich drückt?

SACHS

The wicked shoe! But don't blame me	Der böse Schuh! 's war deine Laun',
You should have tried it on before.	dass du ihn gestern nicht probirt.

EVA

Ah no, my trust was far too great.	Merk' wohl, ich hatt' zu viel Vertrau'n:
The master was not all I thought.	im Meister hab ich mich geirrt.

SACHS

Oh that's a shame! I'll put it right!	Ei, 's thut mir leid! Zeig' her, mein Kind,
Just try to tell me where it's tight.	dass ich dir helfe, gleich geschwind.

EVA

First when I stand it slips away	Sobald ich stehe, will es geh'n:
But when I move it wants to stay.	[22a]doch will ich geh'n, zwingt mich's zu steh'n.

SACHS

Then on the stool here place the shoe,	Hier auf den Schemel streck' den Fuss:
And I will see what I can do.	der üblen Noth ich wehren muss.

(She places one foot on the stool near the table.)

What's wrong with that?	Was ist's mit dem?

EVA

You see, too broad!	Ihr seht, zu weit!

SACHS

Child, that is only vanity;	Kind, das ist pure Eitelkeit:
The shoe fits tight.	Der Schuh ist knapp.

EVA

I told you that!	Das sag' ich ja:
That's why it presses my toes so hard.	drum drückt er mir die Zehen da.

SACHS

Here left?	Hier links?

EVA

No, right.	Nein, rechts.

SACHS

Here at the heel?	Wohl mehr am Spann?

EVA

More on the instep.	Mehr hier am Hacken.

SACHS

What . . . there as well?	Kommt der auch dran?

EVA

Ah, Master! Do you know better than I	Ach Meister! Wüsstet ihr besser als ich,
Where the shoe hurts most?	wo der Schuh mich drückt?

SACHS

I wonder why,	Ei, 's wundert mich
If it's too broad, it still pinches you so!	dass er zu weit, und doch drückt überall?

EVA

Ah!	Ah!

(Walther, in magnificent knightly dress, enters by the inner door, and stands there spell-bound at the sight of Eva. Eva utters a slight cry and remains in the same position, her foot on the stool, looking at Walther. Sachs, bending down before her, has not noticed Walther's entrance.)

Aha! 'Tis here! Now the reason I know. [25]	Aha! hier sitzt's! Nun begreif' ich den Fall!
Child, you are right: something is wrong.	Kind, du hast recht: 's stack in der Naht: –
Be patient, to mend it won't take long;	nun warte, dem Uebel schaff' ich Rath.
Stay where you are; I'll work with the shoe	Bleib' nur so stehn; ich nehm' dir den Schuh
On the last for a moment, your pain will	eine Weil' auf den Leisten: dann lässt er
soon pass.	dir Ruh'!

(Sachs has gently drawn Eva's shoe from her foot; she remains in the same position, while he takes the shoe to the work-table and works at it as though he notices nothing else.)

Always cobbling, that now is my fate,	Immer Schustern! das ist nun mein Loos;
By night, by day, both early and late.	des Nachts, des Tags – komm' nicht davon los!
Child, now hear what plan I have in mind	Kind, hör' zu! Ich hab's überdacht,
That all these hours of hard work may end.	was meinem Schustern ein Ende macht:
Why should I not be your suitor today?	am Besten, ich werbe doch noch um dich;
Some reward as a poet I'd gain that way.	da gewänn' ich doch 'was als Poet für mich! –
You pay no heed? Come speak up clear;	Du hörst nicht drauf? – So sprich doch jetzt!
You know quite well that was your idea!	Hast mir's ja selbst in den Kopf gesetzt? –
Oh well! I see! – "Stick to your shoes!"	Schon gut! – ich merk'! – Mach' deinen Schuh!
Lately I heard a most wonderful song!	Säng' mir nur wenigstens Einer dazu!
Only today it charmed my ear!	Hörte heut' gar ein schönes Lied: –
Ah, if only a third verse I could hear.	wem dazu ein dritter Vers gerieth'!

WALTHER
(gazing at Eva in rapture)

"Lured from their dances the stars glided [7] down,	"Weilten die Sterne im lieblichen Tanz?
New light so clear	So licht und klar
Shone in her hair;	im Lockenhaar,
On her attending,	vor allen Frauen
Beauty lending,	hehr zu schauen,
And round her head there shone	lag ihr mit zartem Glanz

112

A starry crown.
Wonder on wonder revealed to me there;
A twofold morn
Now seemed to dawn;
Her eyes in glory
Shone before me,
Those eyes outshone the sun
With radiance pure and rare.

Hallowed the scene,
That met my ever wondering gaze.
The sunlight garland shed its rays,
The first pale glimmer was then ablaze.
Loving and mild,
Her hand wove its leaves round my head:
Where love has bound me,
There fame has crowned me:
I drink from radiant eyes
All joys of paradise,
In love's dream."

ein Sternenkranz. –
Wunder ob Wunder nun bieten sich dar:
zwiefachen Tag
ich grüssen mag;
denn gleich zwei'n Sonnen
reinster Wonnen,
der hehrsten Augen Paar
nahm ich da wahr. –

Huldreichstes Bild,
dem ich zu nahen mich erkühnt:
den Kranz, vor zweier Sonnen Strahl
zugleich verblichen und ergrünt,
minnig und mild,
sie flocht ihn um das Haupt dem Gemahl.
Dort Huld-geboren,
nun Ruhm-erkoren,
giesst Paradiesische Lust
sie in des Dichters Brust –
im Liebestraum." –

SACHS

(He has brought back the shoe during the last verse of Walther's song and fits it on Eva's foot.)

Now child! That is a Mastersong.
Such songs are heard now in my own house.
Let's see, now perhaps the shoe is right?
I really think
My work is now over!
Just try, stand up! Say, how is it now?

Lausch', Kind! das ist ein Meisterlied:
derlei hörst du jetzt bei mir singen.
Nun schau', ob dabei mein Schuh gerieth?
Mein' endlich doch
es thät' mir gelingen?
Versuch's! tritt auf! – Sag', drückt er dich noch?

(Eva, who has stood motionless as if enchanted, gazing and listening, bursts passionately into tears; sobbing, she embraces Sachs, her head on his breast. Walther approaches them; he presses Sachs's hand. Sachs at length gains control of himself and tears himself moodily away, and so leaves Eva involuntarily leaning on Walther's shoulder.) [32]

SACHS
[32, 11]

The life of a cobbler's nothing but woe!

And were I not a poet too,
Henceforth I'd never make a shoe!
No rest, never free, to all a slave!
Too tight for this one, for that one too loose!
From every quarter nought but abuse.
It flaps
Perhaps,
Or nips,
Or grips!
The cobbler must have skill unending,
Patch up what's in need of a mending.
And if he be a poet too,
For that not a moment of peace will he know;

Should he by chance a widower be,
A fool he must be, all agree;
The youngest maidens, when wooers fail,
Expect him to listen to their tale;
He sees the trap, but if he does not,
All one if he agrees or not.
And then if he smells of pitch,
They call him fool, rascal and wretch.
Ah! Most of all for my prentice I grieve;
For no heed to me will he pay:
For Lene's driving him out of his wits,

And she stuffs his stomach all day.
Now devil take him for this delay!

Hat man mit dem Schuhwerk nicht seine Noth!
Wär' ich nicht noch Poet dazu,
ich machte länger keine Schuh'!
Das ist eine Müh' und Aufgebot!
Zu weit dem Einem, dem Andern zu eng;
von allen Seiten Luft und Gedräng':
da klappt's
da schlappt's
hier drückt's
da zwickt's!
Der Schuster soll auch alles wissen,
flicken was nur immer zerrissen;
und ist er gar Poet dazu,
so lässt man am End' ihm auch da kein' Ruh':
doch ist er erst noch Wittwer gar,
zum Narren macht man ihn fürwahr;
die jüngsten Mädchen, ist Noth am Mann
begehren, er hielte um sie an;
versteht er sie, versteht er sie nicht,
all eins ob ja, ob nein er spricht:
am Ende riecht er doch nach Pech,
und gilt für dumm, tückisch und frech!
Ei, 's ist mir nur um den Lehrbuben leid;
der verliert mir allen Respect;
die Lene macht ihn schon nicht recht gescheit,
dass aus Topf' und Tellern er leckt!
Wo Teufel er jetzt wieder steckt?

EVA
(as she pulls Sachs back and again draws him to her)
[32]

O Sachs! My friend! So kind thou art!	O Sachs! mein Freund! Mein theurer Mann!
How shall I praise thy noble heart?	Wie ich dir Edlem lohnen kann!
Thy love alone has taught me, [37]	Was ohne deine Liebe,
What were I but for thee?	was wär' ich ohne dich,
A child now would I still be,	ob je auch Kind ich bliebe,
Had thou now not wakened me.	erwecktest du mich nicht?
Through thee my wisdom	Durch dich gewann ich
I have won;	Was man preis't,
Through thee my spirit	durch dich ersann ich
I have known;	was ein Geist!
Through thee I wake,	Durch dich erwacht',
Through thee I make	durch dich nur dacht'
Me noble, brave and true;	ich edel, frei und kühn:
Through thee I'm born anew!	due liessest mich erblüh'n! –
Dear Master, though I've wounded you,	O lieber Meister! schilt mich nur!
Yet I know that my heart was true,	Ich war doch auf der rechten Spur:
And if my soul gave voice,	denn, hatte ich die Wahl,
And were my heart my own;	nur dich erwählt' ich mir:
Then thou would'st be my choice,	du warest mein Gemahl,
The prize thine alone.	den Preis nur reicht' ich nur dir! –
But now I feel a power	Doch nun hat's mich gewählt,
That tears my will apart	zu nie gekannter Qual:
And were I wed this hour,	und werd' ich heut' vermählt,
All choice would be in vain:	so war's ohn' alle Wahl!
To stem the torrent in my heart!	Das war ein Müssen, war ein Zwang!
You dearest Master, would not dare.	Euch selbst, mein Meister, wurde bang.

SACHS

My child, [37]	Mein Kind:
Of Tristan and Isolde,	von Tristan und Isolde
A grievous tale I know:	kenn' ich ein traurig Stück:
Hans Sachs was wise and would not	Hans Sachs war klug und wollte
Endure King Marke's woe.	nichts von Herrn Marke's Glück. –
'Twas time I found the man to wed	's war Zeit, dass ich den Rechten fand:
Or else I too would have lost my head.	wär' sonst am End' doch hineingerannt! –
Aha! Now Magdalene is about;	Aha! da streicht die Lene schon um's Haus.
Come along! Ho! David! Time to come out!	Nur herein! – He, David! Kommst nicht heraus?

(Magdalene, dressed for the festival, enters. David, also dressed and decked out with flowers and ribbons, comes out of the room at the same time.)

The witnesses here, a christening's at hand!	Die Zeugen sind da, Gevatter zur Hand
So, for the naming. All take your stand!	jetzt schnell zur Taufe; nehmt euren Stand!

(All look at him in surprise.)

A child has been created, [8,1a]	Ein Kind ward hier geboren;
Let its name now here be stated.	jetzt sei ihm ein Nam' erkoren!
This is by use the Masters' right,	So ist's nach Meister-Weis' und Art,
For when a Mastersong is brought to light,	wenn eine Meisterweise geschaffen ward:
The song by a goodly name they call,	dass die einen guten Namen trag',
By which henceforth 'tis known to all.	dran Jeder sie erkennen mag. –
Now know, worthy people, who hear me,	Vernehmt respectable Gesellschaft,
Why I call you near me.	was euch hierher zur Stell'schafft! –
Since a Mastersong was fashioned newly,	Eine Meisterweise ist gelungen,
And by Sir Walther was sung before us duly;	von Junker Walther gedichtet und gesungen;
He asks if Eva and I would rather	der jungen Weise lebender Vater
Attend him as godmother and godfather.	lud mich und die Pognerin zum Gevatter:
Since to his song we both have listened	weil wir die Weise wohl vernommen,
And all have come that it may be christened.	sind wir zur Taufe hierher gekommen.
That we who have heard attest its fitenss,	Auch dass wir zur Handlung Zeugen haben,
Let David and Lene now stand to witness.	ruf' ich Jungfer Lene, und meinen Knaben:
But as no prentice a witness may be,	doch da's zum Zeugen kein Lehrbube thut,
And David today sang right well to me,	und heut' auch den Spruch er gesungen gut,

A journeyman I will make of him here.	so mach' ich den Burschen gleich zum Gesell';
Kneel David now and take this on the ear.	knie' nieder, David, und nimm' diese Schell'!

(David kneels; Sachs gives him a smart box on the ear.)

Arise, "my man", this blow don't forget, [1]	Steh' auf, Gesell! und denk an den Streich;
A christening it will fix in your pate.	du merkst die dabei die Taufe zugleich! –
If not well done, no blame is ours;	Fehlt sonst noch 'was, uns Keiner drum schilt:
Who knows how the need for a christening arose?	wer weiss, ob's nicht gar einer Nothtaufe gilt.
That the song's good fortune may not be broken	Dass die Weise Kraft behalte zum Leben,
By me, then let its name now be spoken.	will ich nur gleich den Namen ihr geben: –
The "Heavenly Morning Dream Love Story;"	"die selige Morgentraumdeut-Weise"
So be it named to its Master's glory.	sei sie genannt zu des Meisters Preise. –
Now strong may it grow and win each heart,	Nun wachse sie gross, ohn' Schad' und Bruch:
And now let the godmother play her part.	die jüngste Gevatterin spricht den Spruch.

(He moves from the middle of the semi-circle which they have formed around him, so that Eva now stands in the centre.)

EVA

Radiant as the dawning	Selig, wie die Sonne
That enchants my sight,	meines Glückes lacht,
So this lovely morning	Morgen voller Wonne,
Promises delight.	selig mir erwacht!
Dream of endless glory,	Traum der höchsten Hulden,
Heavenly morning glow:	himmlisch Morgenglüh'n!
Who can tell the story?	Deutung euch zu schulden,
Who thy meaning show?	selig süss Bemüh'n!
In this melody pure and tender,	Einer Weise mild und hehr,
There lies a message of gladness	sollt's es hold gelingen,
And it eases my heart's sweet burden	meines Herzens süss Beschwer
Mingling joy with this strange sadness.	deutend zu bezwingen.
Is it but a morning dream?	Ob es nur ein Morgentraum?
I hardly dare to hear its theme.	Selig deut' ich mir es kaum.
But this melody	Doch die Weise,
Confided gently	was sie leise
To me here,	mir vertraut,
A quiet theme,	im stillen Raum,
Bright and clear,	hell und laut,
In the Masters's Guild shall rise,	in der Meister vollem Kreis,
There to win you the highest prize.	deute sie den höchsten Preis!

WALTHER

Love alone, so pure and noble	Deine Liebe, rein und hehr,
Has brought me sudden gladness,	liess es mir gelingen,
Easing all my pain,	meines Herzens süss Beschwer
A joy that mingles with sadness.	deutend zu bezwingen.
Is it still the morning dream?	Ob es noch der Morgentraum?
Dare I think what it may mean?	Selig deut' ich mir es kaum.
What this melody	Doch die Weise,
Once again to me	Was sie leise
Confides	dir vertraut
In stillness here	im stillen Raum,
Bright and clear,	hell und laut,
In the Masters's Guild shall rise,	in der Meister vollem Kreis,
There to win me the highest prize.	werbe sie um höchsten Preis!

SACHS

To this lovely child I long	Vor dem Kinde lieblich hehr,
Now to sing of gladness,	mocht' ich gern wohl singen;
But must hide my heart's sweet pain	doch des Herzens süss Beschwer

Hide my tender sadness.	galt es zu bezwingen.
Such a wondrous morning dream;	's war ein schöner Abendtraum:
Dare I think what it may mean?	daran zu deuten wag' ich kaum.
But this melody	Diese Weise,
Once again	was sie leise
So gently confides	mir vertraut
In the stillness here,	im stillen Raum,
Makes it clear.	sagt mir laut:
Love of youth, that never dies,	auch der Jugend ew'ges Reis
Blooms only through the poet's prize.	grünt nur durch des Dichters Preis.

DAVID

Is this a vision or a dream?	Wach' oder träum' ich schon so früh?
I cannot tell what it may mean.	Das zu erklären macht mir Müh'.
Are my senses so deceived?	's ist wohl nur ein Morgentraum:
What I see I can't believe.	was ich seh', begreif' ich kaum.
I no longer	Ward zur Stelle
An apprentice,	gleich Geselle?
She my bride?	Lene Braut?
Before the altar	Im Kirchenraum
At my side?	wir getraut?
Now my heart in answer cries	's geht der Kopf mir, wie im Kreis,
"Win the Master's prize!"	dass ich bald gar Meister heiss'!

MAGDALENE

Is this a vision or a dream?	Wach' oder träum' ich schon so früh?
I cannot tell what it may mean.	Das zu erklären macht mir Müh':
Are my senses so deceived?	's ist wohl nur ein Morgentraum?
What I see I can't believe.	Was ich seh', begreif' ich kaum!
He no longer	Er zur Stelle
An apprentice,	gleich Geselle?
I, his bride,	Ich die Braut?
Before the altar	Im Kirchenraum
At his side?	wir getraut?
Ah! I know it! My heart sighs	Ja, wahrhaftig! 's geht: wer weiss?
"He as Master shall rise."	Bald ich wohl Frau Meist'rin heiss'!

SACHS
(turning to the others)
[7]

Now let's be off! Your father greet!	Jetzt All' am Fleck! Den Vater grüss'!
Off to the field! There shall we meet.	Auf, nach der Wies' schnell auf die Füss'!

(Eva tears herself away from Sachs and Walther and leaves the house with Magdalene.)

Now! Walther come! You must be brave!	Nun, Junker! Kommt! habt frohen Muth! –
David, my man! See that all is safe!	David, Gesell'! Schliess' den Laden gut!

As Sachs and Walther go together into the street and David starts to lock up the shop doors, the curtain falls. When the music has gradually swelled up to the biggest climax the |curtain rises and the scene has changed. [23, 34, 1b]

Scene Five. *The stage now represents an open meadow; in the distance is the city of Nuremberg. The Pegnitz winds across the plain; the narrow river can be crossed here. Boats gaily decorated with flags continually carry parties of burghers of the different guilds with their wives and families over to the banks of the meadow. A raised stand with benches on it adorned with the banners of those who have already arrived; as the scene opens, the standard-bearers of other guilds also place their banners against the Singer's dais, so that it is finally enclosed on three sides by them. All around the open space are tents with every kind of refreshment. In front of the tents there is much merry-making: Burghers and their families sit in groups round them. The prentices of the Mastersingers, in holiday dress, finely decked out* *with ribbons and flowers and carrying slender wands which are also decorated, carry out their jobs as heralds and stewards in high spirits. They receive new arrivals on the bank, arrange them in procession and accompany them to the dais. The standard-bearer leaves his banner there and the burghers and journeymen disperse among the tents. Amongst the guilds to arrive, the following are particularly noticeable.*

THE SHOEMAKERS
(as they march past)

Saint Crispin,	Sankt Crispin,
Saint Crispin!	lobet ihn!
He was a holy man,	War gar ein heilig Mann,
Did all a cobbler can.	zeigt was ein Schuster kann.
The poor then had a merry time;	Die Armen hatten gute Zeit,
They all wore well-made shoes;	macht' ihnen warme Schuh':
If leather lacked, he turned to crime,	und wenn ihm Keiner Leder leiht,
And stole what he could use.	so stahl er sich's dazu.
A cobbler's conscience is not queasy,	Der Schuster hat ein weit Gewissen,
And little makes him feel uneasy;	macht Schuhe selbst mit Hindernissen;
When from the tanner skin we get,	und ist vom Gerber das Fell erst weg,
Then beat, beat, beat!	dann streck'! streck'! streck'!
Leather serves but to shoe our feet.	Leder taugt nur am rechten Fleck,

(*The Town watchmen appear with trumpets and drums, followed by the Town-pipers, Lute-makers and journeymen with toy instruments.*)

THE TAILORS

When Nuremberg a siege withstood,	Als Nürenberg belagert war,
And famine filled the land,	und Hungersnoth sich fand,
We would have lost our town for good,	wär, Stadt und Volk verdorben gar,
Without a tailor to hand.	war nicht ein Schneider zur Hand,
Boldly then this trick he planned.	der Muth hat und Verstand:
In a goatskin safe, himself he sews,	hat sich in ein Bockfell eingenäht,
On the wall to take a walk he goes,	auf dem Stadtwall da spazieren geht,
And there so gaily springing,	und macht wohl seine Sprünge
He sets the welkin ringing.	gar lustig guter Dinge.
The foe in terror then retreat,	Der Feind, der sieht's und zieht vom Fleck:
The Devil dances through the street,	der Teufel hol' die Stadt sich weg,
Where goats yet so merrily bleat bleat bleat!	hat's drin noch so lustige Meck-meck-meck!
Bleat! Bleat! Bleat!	Meck! Meck! Meck!
Who'd think that a tailor would have such wit?	Wer glaubt's, dass ein Schneider im Bockesteck'!

THE BAKERS
(coming on with their banner flying)

Famine dread! Famine dread!	Hungersnoth! Hungersnoth!
From that may God defend us!	Das ist ein gräulich Leiden!
Bakers must bring us our daily bread,	Gäb' euch die Bäcker kein täglich Brod,
Or hunger soon would end us.	müsst' alle Welt verscheiden.
Wheat, wheat, wheat,	Beck! Beck! Beck!
Makes the bread we eat;	Täglich auf dem Fleck!
So hunger we defeat!	Nimm uns den Hunger weg!

(*A decorated boat arrives full of young girls in beautifully embroidered folk costume. The prentices run to the bank.*) [15]

PRENTICES

Look here! Look here! Maidens from Fürth!	Herr Je! Herr Je! Mädel von Fürth!
Town-pipers, play! And make us gay.	Stadtpfeifer, spielt! dass's lustig wird!

(*The prentices lift the girls out of the boat. The point of the dance that follows is that the prentices apparently only wish to bring the girls to the open space, although the journeymen keep trying to seize the girls, and the prentices try to take them somewhere else, so that they dance around the whole stage, continually delaying their original purpose in good-natured fun.*)

(Coming forward from the landing stage, he looks disapprovingly at the dance.)

You dance? Look out if the Masters see you!   Ihr tanzt? Was werden die Meister sagen?
(The prentices make fun of him.)

Don't care? – Well then, make room   Hört nicht? – Lass' ich mir's auch
  for me too.   behagen!
(He seizes a pretty girl and joins the dance with great enjoyment.)

PRENTICES
(making signs to David)

David! Your Lene looks on!   David! die Lene! die Lene sieht zu!

(David, startled, quickly lets the girl go. The prentices immediately dance in a circle around her. David does not see Lene anywhere and he realises that he has been fooled; breaking through the circle, he seizes the girl and dances on more ardently.)

DAVID

Ah! Stop fooling now and leave me   Ach! lasst mich mit euren Possen in
  alone!   Ruh'!

(The prentices try to pull the girl away from him; he always manages to evade them, so that they repeat the business of dancing around the stage as before.)

JOURNEYMEN, PRENTICES

The Mastersingers! The Mastersingers!   Die Meistersinger! die Meistersinger!

DAVID

Good Lord! – Goodbye, you pretty   Herr Gott! – Ade, ihr hübschen Dinger!
  creatures!

(He gives the girl an ardent kiss and tears himself away. The prentices immediately stop dancing and hurry to the bank, where they line up to receive the Mastersingers: the crowd makes way for them. At the landing-place the Mastersingers prepare for a grand procession and then walk forward to take their places on the stand. First Kothner, as standard-bearer, then Pogner, leading Eva by the hand. She is accompanied by richly-dressed maidens; among them is Magdalene. Then follow the other Mastersingers. At the sight of the banner, painted to show King David with his harp, the people cheer and wave their hats. When Eva, surrounded by her maidens, has taken the place of honour, decorated with flowers, and Kothner has placed his banner – the tallest of all among the other banners – and everyone else is in his place (the Masters on the benches, the journeymen standing behind them) the prentices march to the platform and turn to the people.) [1, 3]

PRENTICES

Silentium! Silentium!   [3]   Silentium! Silentium!
Speak no word, let no sound be heard!   Macht kein Reden und kein Gesumm'!

(Sachs rises and comes forward. When they see him, all press forward and burst into loud cries of acclamation, waving their hats.)

PEOPLE

Ha! Sachs! 'Tis Sachs!   Ha! Sachs! 's ist Sachs!
See! Master Sachs!   Seht! Meister Sachs!
Begin! Begin! Begin!   Stimmt an! Stimmt an! Stimmt an!

(Everyone – except Sachs joins in this verse, taking parts according to their voices. All those sitting stand up; the men take off their hats. Beckmesser, unobserved by the people because he is hidden behind the other Masters, is busy trying to learn his song by heart.)

PEOPLE

'Awake! The dawn of day draws near: [33]   'Wach' auf, es nahet gen den Tag,
From green depths of the woods I hear   ich hör singen im grünen Hag
A soul-enchanting nightingale;   ein wonnigliche Nachtigal
His voice resounds o'er hill and dale;   ihr Stimm' durchklinget Berg und Thal:
The night sinks down in western skies,   die Bacht neigt sich zum Occident,
The day from eastern realms doth rise,   der Tag geht auf von Orient,
The red glow of the dawn awakes   die rothbrünstige Morgenröth'
And through the dusky cloud-bank   her durch die trüben Wolken geht.' –
  breaks.'
     Hail Sachs! Hans Sachs!   Heil Sachs! Hans Sachs!
     Hail Nuremberg's poet Sachs!   [1b, 3]   Hail Nürnberg's theurem Sachs!

SACHS

(Who, deep in thought, has been gazing motionless over the heads of the crowd, at last turns his kindly gaze on them and begins in a voice at first choked with emotion.)

[32]

Words light to you bow me to earth:	Euch wird es leicht, mir macht ihr's schwer,
Such praise is far beyond my worth.	gebt ihr mir Armen zu viel Ehr':
Only one hope now I have,	such' vor der Ehr' ich zu besteh'n,
That I prove worthy of your love.	ei's, mich von euch geliebt zu seh'n!
Already honour you did pay	Schon grosse Ehr' ward mir erkannt,
By naming me speaker for today.	ward heut' ich zum Spruchsprecher ernannt:
	und was mein Spruch euch künden soll,
So hear my speech and heed it well!	glaubt, das ist hoher Ehren voll!
I shall a tale of honour tell.	
Our art I know you highly prize, [14]	Wenn ihr die Kunst so hoch schon ehrt,
It serves to bring you pleasure,	da galt es zu beweisen,
But we who love it in true wise	dass, wer ihr selbst gar angehört,
Hold Art beyond all praise.	sie schätzt ob allen Preisen.
A Master rich, a man of pride,	Ein Meister, reich und hochgemuth,
Will show the love he professes;	der will heut' euch das zeigen:
His daughter fair, his heart's delight,	sein Töchterlein, sein höchstes Gut,
And all that he possesses,	mit allem Hab und Eigen,
He offers this before you all	dem Singer, der im Kunstgesang
To him on whom the choice shall fall;	vor allem Volk den Preis errang,
To prove that art alone	als höchsten Preises Kron'
Can win the highest crown.	er bietet das zum Lohn.
So hark ye now to what I cry.	Darum so hört, und stimmt mir bei:
The poets all are free to try.	die Werbung steht dem Dichter frei.
Ye Masters who will sing today, [14]	Ihr Meister, die ihr's euch getraut,
To you before all folk I say:	euch ruf' ich's vor dem Volke laut:
Think well how rare a prize is here,	erwägt der Werbung selt'nen Preis,
That all may surely bring her	und wem sie soll gelingen,
A heart and voice both pure and clear,	dass der sich rein und edel weiss,
As suitor and as singer.	im Werben, wie im Singen,
Let this your hearts embolden;	will er das Reis erringen,
That never in present times or olden,	dass nie bei Neuen, noch bei Alten
Was crown so nobly high upholden,	ward je so herrlich hoch gehalten,
As by this maiden tender;	als von der lieblich Reinen,
May fate from harm defend her,	die niemals soll beweinen,
That Nuremberg her voice may raise [23]	dass Nürenberg mit höchstem Werth
For Art, and in her Masters' praise!	die Kunst und ihre Meister ehrt.

(Great and general commotion. Sachs goes up to Pogner.)

POGNER

(pressing Sachs's hand with emotion) [23,34,14,15]

O Sachs, my friend! What thanks I owe!	O Sachs! Mein Freund! Wie dankenswerth!
The weight upon my heart you know.	Wie wisst ihr, was mein Herz beschwert!

SACHS

You ventured much, but who can tell?	's war viel gewagt! Jetzt habt nur Muth!

(Beckmesser, to whom Sachs now turns, has been continually taking the poem from his pocket and trying to learn it by heart, often in despair wiping the sweat from his brow.)

Now Marker! Say, d'you feel well?	Herr Merker! Sagt, wie steht es? Gut?

BECKMESSER

Oh! What a song! It sounds so strange,	O, dieses Lied! – Werd' nicht draus klug,
And yet I've studied it enough.	und hab' doch dran studirt genug!

SACHS

My friend, you are not forced to choose it.	Mein Freund, 's ist euch nicht aufgezwungen.

BECKMESSER

With mine all is over, I cannot use it.	Was hilft's? – Mit dem meinen ist doch versungen!
The fault was yours! Help me then to win:	's war eure Schuld! – Jetzt seid hübsch für mich!
To leave me now would be a crime!	's wär' schändlich, liesset ihr mich im Stich!

119

SACHS

| I thought you'd give up. | Ich dächt', ihr gäbt's auf. |

BECKMESSER

And why, I pray?	Warum nicht gar?
The others will not stand in my way;	Die Andern sing' ich alle zu paar'!
If you do not sing.	Wenn ihr nur nicht singt.

SACHS

| That we shall see! | So seht, wie's geht. |

BECKMESSER

| The song by no-one will be understood; | Das Lied! – bin's sicher – zwar Keiner versteht: |
| But I bank upon your favour with the crowd. | doch bau' ich auf eure Popularität. |

(*The prentices have hastily heaped up in front of the Mastersingers' platform a little mound of turf, beaten solid and strewn with flowers.*)

SACHS

| Well then, if Masters and folk agree, | Nun denn, wenn's Meistern und Volk beliebt, |
| To hear the singers we now are free. | Zum Wettgesang man den Anfang giebt. |

KOTHNER
(*advancing*)

Unmarried Masters, all be prepared!	Ihr ledig' Meister, macht euch bereit!
The eldest man shall first be heard.	Der Aeltest' sich zuerst anlässt: –
Friend Beckmesser, now begin: 'tis time.	Herr Beckmesser, ihr fangt an, 's ist Zeit!

(*The prentices lead Beckmesser to the small mound in front of the platform. Beckmesser stumbles on to it and stands tottering and insecure.*) [1a]

BECKMESSER

| The devil! How rickety! Now make it firm! | Zum Teufel! Wie wackelig! Macht das hübsch fest! |

(*The prentices laugh among themselves and ram down the turf.*)

PEOPLE
(*nudging one another*)

What? He? He woos? Surely she'll refuse him!	Wie der? Der wirbt? Scheint mir nicht der Rechte!
In the maiden's place I would not choose him!	An der Tochter Stell' ich den nicht möchte. –
He cannot keep his feet!	Er kann nicht 'mal stehn:
How could he win her hand?	Wie wird's mit dem gehn? –
Be still! For he's a skilful Master!	Seid still! 's ist gar ein tücht'ger Meister!
He is the town clerk, Master Beckmesser!	Stadtschreiber ist er: Beckmesser heisst er.
Lord! What a fool!	Gott ist der dumm!
He'll tumble soon.	Er fällt fast um! –
Still! And make no jest!	[1b] Still! macht keinen Witz;
He has in council vote and seat.	der hat in Rathe Stimm und Sitz.

PRENTICES

| Silentium! Silentium! | [3] Silentium! Silentium! |
| Speak no word! Let no sound be heard! | Macht kein Reden und kein Gesumm'! |

KOTHNER

| Now begin! | Fanget an! |

BECKMESSER
(*who has finally secured a firm footing on the mound, bows first to the Masters, then to the people and then to Eva, at whom, when she turns away, he blinks with embarrassment; he tries to calm his uneasiness by a prelude on the lute*)

"Bathing in sunlight at dawning of day,	[36] "Morgen ich leuchte in rosigem Schein,
With bosom bare,	voll Blut und Duft
To greet the air;	geht schnell die Luft; –
With beauty glowing,	wohl bald gewonnen!

120

Faster snowing;
A garden roundelay
Wearied my way."

wie zerronnen, –
im Garten lud ich ein –
garstig und fein." –

MASTERSINGERS
(*softly to each other*)

Ah! What is that? He's lost his senses!
But where has he ever discovered such fancies?

Mein! was ist das? Ist er von Sinnen?
Woher mocht' er solche Gedanken gewinnen?

PEOPLE
(*softly to each other*)

Curious! D'you hear? What roundelay?
Can that be right? How can that be?

Sonderbar! Hört ihr's? Wen lud er ein?
Verstand man recht? Wie kann das sein?

BECKMESSER
(*He secretly pulls out the verses and hurriedly looks at them before pocketing the paper again.*)

"Sigh for the bard, on a tree did he rise,
  A golden sore
  Its branches tore,
  With midges thronging
  Broke my longing,
  When, dark and bare, the prize
  Hooked on my eyes!"

"Wohn' ich erträglich im selbigen Raum,
  hol' Gold und Frucht –
  Bleisaft und Wucht:
  mich holt am Pranger –
  der Verlanger, –
  auf luft'ger Steige kaum –
  häng' ich am Baum." –

(*He totters again, and tries in vain to sneak another look at the paper. His head begins to swim and he perspires with anxiety.*)

MASTERSINGERS

What is the meaning? Is he gone mad?
His song is utter nonsense!

Was soll das heissen? Ist er nur toll?
Sein Lied ist ganz von Unsinn voll!

PEOPLE

Dainty wooer! His due he soon will get.
He'll end on the gallows. Yes, that is clear.

Schöner Werber! Der find't sein Lohn:
bald hängt er am Galgen; man sieht ihn schon.

BECKMESSER
(*He tries to pull himself together with an effort of despair and rage, but he becomes ever more confused.*)

"What is her name?
What radiant thunder clearly pealed?
A woman's hair in fashion dressed:
With clear immortal air it swelled.
  Bridling she came,
And folded me there in a chest;
  Intently gazing,
  Her hound was grazing
And gleaned the roots old and new:
She sowed the space with rue,
  The seed of strife!"

"Heimlich mir graut –
weil hier es munter will hergeh'n: –
an meiner Leiter stand ein Weib, –
sie schämt' und wollt' mich nicht beseh'n.
  Bleich wie ein Kraut –
umfasert mir Hanf meinen Leib; –
  die Augen zwinkend –
  der Hund blies winkend –
was ich vor langem verzehrt, –
wie Frucht, so Holz und Pferd –
  vom Lederbaum." –

(*All break out into mocking laughter. Furious, Beckmesser rushes off the mound towards Sachs.*)

BECKMESSER

Accursed cobbler, yours the design!
The song, in truth, is none of mine:
But Sachs, whom ye so much revere,
He wrote the song I sang you here!
Now through his shameful trick I see!
His wretched song he puts on me.

Verdammter Schuster! Das dank' ich dir!
Das Lied, es ist gar nicht von mir:
von Sachs, der hier so hoch verehrt,
von eur'em Sachs ward mir's bescheert!
Mich hat der Schändliche gedrängt,
sein schlechtes Lied mir aufgehängt.

(*He rushes away in fury and is lost in the crowd.*)

PEOPLE

Hey! What can that mean? No-one can conceive it!
The song's by Sachs? None can believe it!

Mein! Was soll das? Jetzt wird's immer bunter!
Von Sachs das Lied? Das nähm' uns doch Wunder!

MASTERSINGERS

Explain, then Sachs! What a disgrace!	Erklärt doch Sachs! Welch ein Skandal!
The song's by you? How strange the case!	Von euch das Lied Welch eig'ner Fall!

SACHS

(who has quietly taken up the paper which Beckmesser threw down)

The song, in truth, is not by me:	Das Lied fürwahr ist nicht von mir:
Friend Beckmesser's wrong, you soon will see.	Herr Beckmesser irrt, wie dort so hier!
So may he himself say where he found it; [21b]	Wie er dazu kam, mag er selbst sagen;
As for me, I dare not boast I wrote it;	doch möcht' ich mich nie zu rühmen wagen,
A song, like this, so fine in thought,	ein Lied, so schön wie dies erdacht,
Never could Hans Sachs have wrought.	sei von mir, Hans Sachs, gemacht.

MASTERSINGERS

What? Fine? All those senseless words?	Wie? schön dies Lied? Der Unsinn-Wust!

PEOPLE

Hear! Sachs makes fun! He says that in jest!	Hört, Sachs macht Spass! Er sagt's zur Lust.

SACHS

I tell you friends, the song is fine,	Ich sag' euch Herr'n, das Lied ist schön:
And it should not take you long to divine	nur ist's auf den ersten Blick zu erseh'n,
That friend Beckmesser sang it wrong.	dass Freund Beckmesser es entstellt.
I swear it, you will like the song,	Doch schwör ich, dass es euch gefällt,
If rightly sung you hear it	wenn richtig die Wort' und Weise
By one who knows its secret;	hier einer säng' im Kreise.
And he who can show he has the key	Und wer das verstünd', zugleich bewies',
Will prove himself the poet,	das er des Liedes Dichter,
A worthy Mastersinger he;	und gar mit Rechte Meister hiess',
All who have ears will know it.	fänd er gerechte Richter.
I am accused, and take my stand:	Ich bin verklagt, und muss besteh'n:
So let me call my witness here to hand.	drum lasst meinen Zeugen mich auserseh'n! –
If one who knows the truth be near,	Ist Jemand hier, der Recht mir weiss,
Let him as witness now appear!	der tret' als Zeug' in diesen Kreis!

(Walther steps forward from the crowd, greets Sachs, and then the Masters and the people in turn, with knightly courtesy. There is a general movement of approval. All remain silent for a short time, observing him.) [5, 16a]

Bear witness, this song is none of mine;	So zeuget, das Lied sei nicht von mir;
And witness, too, the song is fine;	und zeuget auch, dass, was ich hier
That all may agree	hab'von dem Lied gesagt,
My praise was not too free.	zuviel nicht sei gewagt.

MASTERSINGERS

Ah Sachs, your wit is keen!	Ei, Sachs! Gesteht, ihr seid gar fein! –
But you today again will win.	So mag's denn heut geschehen sein.

SACHS

Those rules are best that will stand wear and tear,	Der Regel Güte daraus man erwägt,
And, now and then, exceptions will bear.	dass sie auch 'mal 'ne Ausnahm' verträgt.

PEOPLE

A goodly witness! Proud and bold!	Ein guter Zeuge, schön und kühn!
Methinks, from him some good may come.	Mich dünkt, dem kann 'was Gut's erblüh'n.

SACHS

Masters and folk 'tis your will	Meister und Volk sind gewillt
That my witness now may show his skill.	zu vernehmen, was mein Zeuge gilt.
Sir Walther of Stolzing, sing the song!	Herr Walther von Stolzing, singt das Lied!
Ye Masters, see if he goes wrong.	Ihr Meister, les't, ob's ihm gerieth.

(He gives the verses to Kothner so that he can follow the song.)

| None speaks a word, but all are dumb; | Alles gespannt, 's gibt kein Gesumm', |
| Then we need not call out 'Silentium!' | da rufen wir auch nicht Silentium! |

WALTHER
(*With assurance, he steps firmly on to the mound.*)
[7]

"Warm in the sunlight at dawning of day,	"Morgenlich leuchtend in rosigem Schein,
While blossoms rare	von Blüth' und Duft
Made sweet the air,	geschwellt die Luft,
With beauty glowing	voll aller Wonnen
Past all knowing,	nie ersonnen,
A garden round me lay,	ein Garten lud mich ein, –

(*Kothner, who, with the other Masters, had started to follow the written words of the song, is now deeply moved, and lets the paper drop. They all listen attentively as Walther continues in ecstasy.*)

And there beneath a wondrous tree,	dort unter einem Wunderbaum
With fruit so richly thronging,	von Früchten reich behangen,
My blissful dream revealed to me	zu schau'n in sel'gem Liebestraum,
The goal of all my longing,	was höchstem Lustverlangen
And life's most glorious prize,	Erfüllung kühn verhiess –
A woman fair:	das schönste Weib,
Eva in Paradise!"	Eva im Paradies."

PEOPLE
(*murmuring softly*)

| Who would have thought it? Who could have known? | Das ist'was And'res! Wer hätt's gedacht? |
| How much lies hid in words and 'tone'! | Was doch recht Wort und Vortrag macht! |

MASTERSINGERS
(*murmuring softly*)

| Ah yes, I see, 'tis another thing | Ja wohl! Ich merk'! 's ist ein ander Ding, |
| If you wrongly or rightly sing. | ob falsche man oder richtig sing! |

SACHS

| Witness indeed! | Zeuge am Ort! |
| Now proceed! | Fahret fort! |

WALTHER

"Darkness had fallen and night closed around;	"Abendlich dämmernd umschloss mich die Nacht;
Alone I strode	auf steilem Pfad
The rugged road	war ich genaht
Where on a mountain	wohl einer Quelle
Rose a fountain	reiner Welle
That lured my steps with its sound:	die lockend mir gelacht:
And there beneath a laurel tree,	dort unter einem Lorbeerbaum,
Where shining stars were showing,	von Sternen hell durchschienen,
In poet's dream there smiled on me,	ich schau' im wachen Dichtertraum,
With holy radiance glowing,	mit heilig holden Mienen
My muse, who from the sacred fount	mich netzend mit dem edlen Nass,
Bedewed my head,	das hehrste Weib –
The Muse of Parnass."	die Muse des Parnass."

PEOPLE
(*murmuring softly*)

| How sweet the strain, how high its theme, | So hold und traut, wie fern es schwebt, |
| And yet it seems to us as though we lived within the dream! | doch ist's als ob man's mit erlebt! |

MASTERSINGERS

| 'Tis strange and daring, that is true; | 's ist kühn und seltsam, das ist wahr: |
| But good are rhymes and singing too! | doch wohlgereimt und singebar. |

SACHS

| Witness true indeed! | Zeuge wohl erkiest! |
| To the end proceed! | Fahret fort, und schliesst! |

WALTHER
(ardently)

"Oh, hallowed day,	"Huldreichster Tag,
On which my poet's dream took flight!	dem ich aus Dichter's Traum erwacht!
That Paradise my vision showed,	Das ich geträumt, das Paradies,
Revealed anew in Heaven's light,	in himmlisch neu verklärter Pracht
Shining now lay;	hell vor mir lag,
And there laughing now a stream the path did show	dahin lachend nun der Quell den Pfad mir wies:
To where in wonder,	die, dort geboren,
In heavenly splendour	mein Herz erkoren,
The garden's maiden so fair,	der Erde lieblichstes Bild,
As Muse before me stood	zur Muse mir geweiht,
In holy calmness there.	so heilig ernst als mild,
That maid I boldly wooed;	ward kühn von mir gefreit,
And there in light of Heaven,	am lichten Tag der Sonnen
The prize of song was given,	durch Sanges Sieg gewonnen
Parnass and Paradise!"	Parnass und Paradies!"

PEOPLE
(softly)

Enchanted by this beauteous dream,	Gewiegt wie in den schönsten Traum,
Scarce can I read its meaning plain.	hör' ich es wohl, doch fass' es kaum.
Grant him his own,	Reich' ihm das Reis
His be the crown.	Sein der Preis!
Right such as his, none here hath shown!	Keiner wie er zu werben weiss!

MASTERSINGERS

Yes, gracious singer, take thine own!	Ja, holder Sänger! Nimm das Reis!
Thy song hath won the Master's crown!	Dein Sang erwarb dir Meisterpreis!

POGNER

O Sachs! Thou bring'st me peace at last:	O Sachs! Dir dank' ich Glück und Ehr'!
Now all my heart's distress is past!	Vorüber nun all' Herzbeschwer!

EVA

No one but you so clear a right has shown!	Keiner wie du so hold zo werben weiss!

Eva has remained outwardly composed and calm, oblivious of all that has happened around her since the beginning of the scene, and she has listened to Walther without moving; but now that at the end both Masters and people express their unfeigned admiration, she rises, advances to the edge of the platform and places the wreath of myrtle and laurel on his brow, as he kneels on the steps. She then leads him to her father, before whom they both kneel. Pogner extends his hands to bless them.

SACHS
(turning to the people and pointing to Walther and Eva)

The witness has been duly tried;	Den Zeugen, denk' es, wählt ich gut:
Are you with Sachs dissatisfied?	tragt ihr Hans Sachs drum üblen Muth?

PEOPLE
(bursting out with shouts of joy)

Hans Sachs! No! That was finely planned!	Hans Sachs! Nein! Das war schön erdacht!
Once more, indeed, your wit the day has gained!	Das habt ihr einmal wieder gut gemacht!

MASTERSINGERS

Up, Master Pogner! 'Tis your right,	Auf, Meister Pogner: Euch zum Ruhm,
Now as a Master to name the knight!	meldet dem Junker sein Meisterthum!

POGNER
(carrying a golden chain with three large medals)

Now take from me King David's shield.	[3] Geschmückt mit König David's Bild,
I make you free of the Masters' Guild!	nehm' ich euch auf in der Meister Gild'.

WALTHER
(refusing the chain impetuously)

Not Master! No!	Nicht Meister! Nein!
One better way to Heaven I know!	Will ohne Meister selig sein!

(He looks tenderly at Eva. All look at Sachs in great perplexity.)

SACHS
(grasping Walther by the hand)

Do not disdain our Masters thus,	[1a]	Verachtet mir die Meister nicht, ✓
But honour well their art!		und erhrt mir ihre kunst!
That which they love and prize the most		Was ihnen hoch zum Lobe spricht,
Has made them take your part.		fiel reichlich euch zur Gunst.
'Twas not your father's name and worth,		Nicht euren Ahnen, noch so werth,
Nor yet your title, wealth or birth;		nicht euren Wappen, Speer, noch Schwert,
It was your poet's art		dass ihr ein Dichter seid,
That won a Master's heart,		ein Meister euch gefreit,
Him must you thank for all your bliss.		dem dankt ihr heut' eu'r höchstes Glück.
So think with thankfulness on this.		Drum, denkt mit Dank ihr d'ran zurück,
Who could an art like ours despise		wie kann die Kunst wohl unwerth sein,
That brings him such a noble prize?		die solche Preise schliesset ein? –
This art our Masters well did guard.	[3]	Dass uns're Meister sie gepflegt,
They knew its true estate		grad' recht nach ihrer Art,
And in its spirit firm they stood,		nach ihrem Sinne treu gehegt,
Thus have they kept it great,		das hat sie ächt bewahrt:
And though not honoured as of old,	[1b]	blieb sie nicht adlig, wie zur Zeit,
When courts and kings its glories told;		wo Höf' und Fürsten sie geweiht,
When strife and turmoil grew,		im Drang der schlimmen Jahr'
Nobly it stood and true:		blieb sie doch deutsch und wahr;
And though our art was honoured less		und wär sie anders nicht geglückt,
Throughout the years of storm and stress,		als wie wo Alles drängt' und drückt'
You see, 'tis highly honoured still.		ihr seht, wie hoch sie blieb in Ehr'!
Then have the Masters done so ill?		Was wollt ihr von den Meistern mehr?
Take heed! Ill times now threaten all;		Habt Acht! Uns drohen üble Streich': –
And if we German folk should fall		zerfällt erst deutsches Volk und Reich,
And foreigners should rule our land		in falscher wälscher Majestät
No king his folk would understand,		kein Fürst dann mehr sein Volk versteht;
And foreign rule and foreign ways		und wälschen Dunst mit wälschen Tand
Would darken all our German days;		sie pflanzen uns in's deutsche Land.
The good and true were soon forgot,		Was deutsch und ächt wüsst' keiner mehr,
Did they not live in Masters' art.		lebt's nicht in deutscher Meister Ehr'.
I say to you,		Drum sag' ich Euch:
Honour your noble Masters,	[5]	ehrt eure deutschen Meister:
Thus you will shun disasters;		dann bannt ihr gute Geister!
If you hold them close to your heart;		Und gebt ihr ihrem Wirken Gunst,
Then may depart		zerging' in Dunst
The fame of ancient Rome		das heil'ge röm'sche Reich,
We have at home		uns bliebe gleich
Our sacred German art!	[1b]	die heil'ge deutsche Kunst!

During the finale Eva takes the wreath from Walther's head and crowns Sachs with it; he takes the chain from Pogner and hangs it around Walther's neck. After Sachs has embraced the pair, Walther and Eva remain one on each side of him leaning on his shoulders. Pogner kneels as if in homage before Sachs. The Mastersingers acclaim Sachs with upraised hands as their leader. While the prentices clap hands and shout and dance, the people wave their hats enthusiastically.

PEOPLE

Honour your noble masters,		Ehrt eure deutschen Mesiter:
Thus you will shun disasters;		dann bannt ihr gute Geister!
If you hold them close to your heart;		Und gebt ihr ihrem Wirken Gunst,
Then may depart		zerging' in Dunst
The fame of ancient Rome,		das heil'ge röm'sche Reich,
We have at home		uns bliebe gleich
Our sacred German art!		die heil'ge deutsche Kunst!
Hail! Sachs! Hans Sachs!	[19]	Heil Sachs! Hans Sachs!
Nuremberg's poet Sachs!		Heil Nürnberg's theurem Sachs!

The curtain falls.

The final scene at Covent Garden in 1930 (Raymond Mander and Joe Mitchenson Theatre Collection)

The final act in Wolfgang Wagner's 1981 Bayreuth production (photo: Festspielleitung Bayreuth)